The *Pawn* Who Would be *Queen*

The Story of Alabama's First National Champions

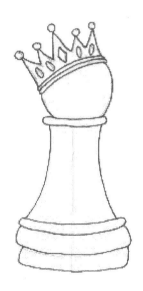

Eric Nager

ERIC NAGER

V18

ISBN: 9781945190452

Pawn Drawing by Aubrey Engeriser

Visit the website: **www.ThePawnWhoWouldBeQueen.com**

Intellect Publishing, LLC
6581 County Road 32, Suite 1195
Point Clear, AL 36564
www.IntellectPublishing.com
Inquiries to: info@IntellectPublishing.com

Reviews

I had the chance to read this book during the 2019 Junior High Chess Nationals in Dallas, where Coach Nager's Bayside Chess Team competed. This book is very well written and it is clear that Coach Nager is extremely passionate about his chess team. As a fellow chess teacher, I appreciated his documented ups and downs and how his team persevered through adversity. 5 star read and I would recommend this to any chess teacher. Go Admirals! –**Alanna Katz**, Co-Founder and Lead Instructor at Growing Minds Chess Academy

The Pawn Who Would be Queen is a fascinating and wonderfully written story told by the coach of a small private school in Alabama that assembled a chess team that went on to win the both the state and national championship. It is a must read for anyone interested in the game of chess, or for that matter *anyone* parent, child, or whomever, who is interested in learning how to overcome obstacles.
 –**Winston Groom**, author of *Forrest Gump*

The Pawn Who Would be Queen, by Eric Nager, provides a comprehensive match by match account of a chess coach's efforts to build a strong competitive scholastic chess team at Bayside Academy near Mobile, Alabama. Nager recounts the challenges, mistakes, and setbacks involved in building a consistent program. The ultimate goal was – and is – to help students develop the skills they need to be successful in life. -**Jerry Nash,** National Chess Education Consultant, Chess in Schools LLC

This is the story of how the greatest game in the world can transform lives with skills that last a lifetime. As told through the eyes of the coach, chess is a level playing field for those who want to succeed through better thinking and decision-making. Bayside is the team that does the unexpected year after year on the national chess scene. Eric explains how he uses his own unique style to channel his passion into his students. Whether it is in business, sports, or life follow the Bayside way of incorporating chess into your world and come out a champion! -**Jim Egerton**, Author of *Business on the Board: How the World's Greatest Game Can Build Better Leaders*

The Pawn Who Would Be Queen is a very inspiring success story of a scholastic chess program in Alabama (which is known more for college football and not so much for chess) which was built by a very passionate and dedicated chess coach. His teams have won countless county and state titles, and even a national championship. This book reminds me of the struggles I faced as a coach. Coach Nager continuously strives for excellence "because nothing else will do." A must-read for anyone who aims to start a brand-new chess program. – **Susan Polgar**, first female grandmaster, World & Olympic Champion, chess coach at Webster University

Author Eric Nager's love of chess began when his dad taught him the game during fourth grade. Years later, Eric went on to coach the first-ever school chess team from Alabama to win a National Championship. This is a quick read—even if you're not a chess player. It is by turns a personal memoir, a chronicle of the growing pains of a program, and a how-to manual for great coaching. And embedded throughout is a hopeful blueprint hinting about all the good that more chess could bring to the children and schools of our world. I first met Eric over ten years ago. As I finished the book, I recalled with a jolt that Eric is not a teacher, not professionally connected with K-12 education in any way. He has coached one team at one small school since 2000 as a classic community volunteer. Although he does now accept an honorarium to cover his persona expenses, the work has been done out of pure love—love for the game, love for the confidence kids get from playing chess well, and especially love for the children and families and school he serves—which is the part of this story that inspires me most. It's a great true-life adventure unfolding at a refreshingly human pace. -**Andrew Clements**, author of *Frindle*

DEDICATION

To Dad who taught me how to play the game; to all my family members, friends, and co-workers who supported me over the years; to all of the opponents we have played – thank you for being there; to all the players, parents, and administrators at Bayside Academy, especially Mrs. Kalaris.

Look at what we accomplished together!

ERIC NAGER

ACKNOWLEDGMENTS

To Ted for inviting me to talk, and to John for listening.

I'd also like to add my thanks to Terry and Southern Capital Services, my employer, for giving me the time to coach.

ERIC NAGER

INTRODUCTION

In the spring of 2016, I gave a talk on my first book, *Checklist for Checkmate: 15 Keys to Building a Successful Team.* Soon after I had lunch with my new friend, John O'Melveny Woods, who attended the talk. He told me, "Eric, your book made some good points, but you did not tell the story about Bayside Academy chess. That's what people want to read: a story about overcoming obstacles."

I had to admit he was right.

The Checklist book was written as a business title for leaders of various types of teams. At the time I wrote it, I did not think that potential readers would be interested in a chess story. But John helped me realize that, strictly speaking, ours in not a chess story. It's the story of an underdog prevailing against the odds over and over again. In fact, one idea I had for the title was *Beating Goliath Every Day,* based on the biblical account of David and Goliath since Bayside Academy, as David, routinely defeats the Goliath of larger schools on an annual basis.

But because chess is the backdrop to this story, a chess analogy for the title is more appropriate. Of all the pieces on the board the lowly pawn is the least powerful, but if it can somehow get to the other side of the board it can become a queen, the most powerful chess piece of all. In that sense, Bayside Academy is symbolized by the pawn and all the success we have enjoyed is the queen.

Of course, the journey to the other side of the board is often tortuous so this book was written to inspire underdogs everywhere to never give up. It was also written to document once and for all our remarkable story and name the names of all those who have had a hand in our success. There have been many books written about athletic successes. This book was also written to stake the claim that academic competitions and championships are every bit as prestigious and important.

What will you get out of this book? Hopefully three things. First, I hope you will be entertained by the story. Second, I hope it will be a lesson for you in perseverance. There have been many hurdles and setbacks in our journey, as there are in all journeys, so I'd like this to be an example for you that, no matter what you are facing, you can do it! Third, I would like this book to convince you that IT IS A GOOD IDEA FOR KIDS TO PLAY CHESS!

Why is this important?

I sincerely believe that if chess were introduced into the national educational curriculum, it would solve many of our academic shortcomings in relatively short order. This theory is based on several facts. One is that many other nations around the world do teach chess as a math subject and have higher standardized test scores in math than the United States. Another is that I have observed chess being taught in the classroom at the third-grade level and that students absolutely love it. The teacher of this class, Jane Allen Hotard, told me she could see how the students were applying the concepts they were learning to other subjects, including art. In other words, chess was making them better students.

Games make learning fun and chess is one of the oldest and most complex games in the world. As life master Robert Haines once told me, "If it had been raining since the beginning of time, and each drop represented a different possible position on the chess board, from the beginning of time until now, we would not have approached the total number of possible positions."

Doesn't that sound like a subject worth studying?

ERIC NAGER

The *Pawn* Who Would be *Queen*

The Story of Alabama's First National Champions

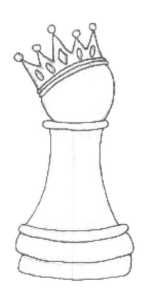

ERIC NAGER

Chapter 1

HOW IT ALL BEGAN

Let's start by playing a word association game. I'll name a state within the United States, and you say the first thing that pops into your head. There is only one ground rule: it has to be a positive association. In other words, if I said New York, you would be prohibited from saying "Yankees."

Are you ready? I'll name the states and then leave a little room, so you can write your answer without looking below first:

FLORIDA

CALIFORNIA

TEXAS

PENNSYLVANIA

ALABAMA

Well, what words did you find? For Florida, I have heard answers such as "beaches," "sunshine," "citrus fruit," "Disney World," etc. What about California, sometimes referred to as the Land of Fruits and Nuts? Good words to associate with that state might be "surfing," "Sequoias," "the Tournament of Roses Parade," and "the entertainment industry."

There are many choices for Texas: "cowboys" (not the football team), "Johnson Space Center," "the San Antonio River Walk," and "barbeque," among others. For Pennsylvania there is "the Liberty Bell," "Hershey chocolate," "Groundhog Day," and "Carnegie Mellon University." With more thought, these lists could be much longer.

But what about Alabama? Probably the most positive association with the state is "college football." The Alabama Crimson Tide has been a national power for 90 years. With no professional sports teams here, college football takes on heightened importance. And, in the aftermath of the American Civil War, the South desperately needed something to lift its collective spirits. I will leave you to look up for yourself the importance of the 1926 Rose Bowl, but after that game, this state has never been the same. Sometimes, dare I say it? There is too much emphasis on football.

In all my years as a chess coach, I have never heard anyone associate Alabama with chess. Maybe this book will help to change that. Interestingly, one of the greatest football players in the history of Alabama loves to play chess: Shaun Alexander. Shaun was a running back with the team in the 1990s and led the Tide to a Southeastern Conference (SEC) championship. He was drafted into the National Football League (NFL) by the Seattle Seahawks, and one year led the league in rushing and led his team to the Super Bowl.

I am told that in Seattle he held a chess contest for the city's children, and he awarded the winner tickets to see him play in the Pro Bowl all-star game in Hawaii. Shaun, if you are reading this, I would love for you to come back to Alabama and address my chess team. My real fantasy if he ever agreed to do this would be for some football coach to come sniffing around the talk and try to get Shaun to address his football team also. My response would be, "Sorry, Coach: Shaun is not here to talk about football. He is here to talk about chess!"

Origins of the Game

Chess is one of the oldest, if not the oldest board game in the world and one of the most popular, played by millions around the globe. The origins are a little murky. Most scholars believe it was invented in India about 1500 years ago, although some believe it was invented in China. From India it spread to Persia, or modern-day Iran, before expanding into Southern Europe. At first it was a slow, plodding game, with today's most powerful piece, the queen, limited to moving one space at a time like the king. However, it is estimated that chess became the modern, attacking game it is today sometime during the 1400s. The first chess World Champion was crowned in the 1880s.

Despite the board being limited in size to eight squares by eight squares, the total possible combinations for positions where pieces can legally move are almost unfathomable. This is what makes the game so great as a teaching tool for analytical thinking, and it is also why it took until the 1990s for a specialized computer to finally defeat the human World Champion. New chess theory continues being developed today. Best of all, whether or not you speak the language of a country you visit, you can always play a game of chess.

Introducing Bayside Academy

Bayside Academy was founded in 1970 as a private, secular academic institution on the beautiful Eastern Shore of Mobile Bay. Its first high school class graduated in 1975, and today the school has an enrollment of about 730 students in grades PK-12. The mission of Bayside Academy is "to educate and develop students who are fully prepared to pursue learning throughout life. These students exhibit high moral standards, a sense of responsibility, respect for self and others, and commitment to excellence in all their endeavors." The chess program is no exception to this mission.

The school is a co-educational, college preparatory day school and Bayside's graduates have gone on to distinguish themselves in the collegiate academic world and beyond. Class sizes are small, allowing the faculty to give individualized attention to the students. Perhaps the most attractive feature of Bayside's values is that Bayside Academy is a family. This value is lived out in practice as the older and younger kids mix together in harmony.

As a private school, you might think that Bayside has certain advantages over public schools in academic-type competitions like chess, and to a certain extent that is true. However, this advantage is more than balanced out by size. In Alabama there are now seven athletic classifications to ensure that in sports, schools only compete against other schools of similar size. There are no such class divisions for chess, and today Bayside is in the 3A athletic classification. This means that we regularly compete against high schools with as many as double the total students that Bayside has in grades K-12.

In addition, Bayside is one of the smaller private schools in our area. Rival McGill-Toolen is 7A, and University Military School (UMS)-Wright is 4A, for example. In other words, every time we compete it is similar to the movie *Hoosiers*. The movie depicts the true story of an Indiana high school basketball team in the 1950s. In their state championship tournament at the time, all schools regardless of size competed in the same event, and the team portrayed in the movie won it all. It was a monumental upset because they were one of the smallest schools ever to win it.

The Mobile-Baldwin County Chess League

My dad taught me to play chess when I was in the fourth grade. I liked the idea of leading an army across the chess board in combat with my opponent. I never thought about this at the time, but one of the rules of chess is that if you get your pawn to the other end of the board, you may redeem it for another queen. By that logic, all pawns are girls, meaning the majority of the total pieces on the board are girls. Talk about an integrated army! At any rate, it was not until tenth grade that I finally beat my dad, and some of the credit goes to the practice I had in our local chess league.

What is today called the Mobile-Baldwin County Chess League began in academic year 1970-71, coincidentally the same year Bayside Academy was founded. The name derives from the two counties in the southwest portion of Alabama that touch the Gulf of Mexico and surround Mobile Bay. In those days, the only schools that competed were high schools and all of the schools were from Mobile except one: Fairhope High School in Baldwin County, my alma mater.

In the early years, the league was dominated by the private schools, with UMS winning the first two years and McGill-Toolen winning six of the next ten. Only in between did the mighty Blount High Leopards of Pritchard rise up to capture four in a row. I was fortunate to play a few games in the league during the final years of the McGill dynasty. My junior high was a feeder school for Fairhope and I was identified as a budding chess player. Some weeks I was able to make it to practice with the team on the high school campus after school.

All the matches were played in Mobile since that is where most all the schools in the league were, and on game day the team would swing by my school and pick me up. It was a great, although somewhat intimidating, experience as a seventh and eighth grader to play high school kids in match play. I was worked into the B team, or junior varsity, where I could get some games under my belt.

I am not sure what his affiliation with the school was, but a long-haired chess enthusiast named Rich Belezza, who owned an old bread delivery truck, drove the team to all the matches and this is the vehicle that pulled into my junior high parking lot to get me. One guy sat on the dashboard with his back to the windshield, one of the side doors may have been open, and there may even have been some smoking. As the wide-eyed, junior high kid, I kept to myself and stayed quiet in the back. A transportation arrangement like this would never fly today, and I am kind of amazed it did even then!

Once we arrived to our matches our teams were good, yet we seemed to perpetually finish third behind McGill and UMS. Kevin Bigbie, Kevin Spriggs, Herbert Cole, Tommy Key, and Tracy Powe were some of the teammates I remember from this time. So was David Adams, who has the distinction of being the first known Bayside Academy student to play competitive chess. Bayside did not have a team at this time, and David would sit in with us as a guest player on occasion.

By the time I reached high school, the chess team had cleaned up its act. Rich had moved on to Atlanta and our highly organized and no-nonsense faculty sponsor was Dawn Malec. One holdover player from the previous era was Spencer Davis who returned for his senior year. I had the honor of playing second board behind him as a sophomore. The good McGill teams were gone, but the new nemesis was Theodore High School, a public school from western Mobile County.

We finished second to Theodore that year, but it was Fairhope's best showing ever to that time, and Spencer won the Morphy Award for the best player in our league: the first time someone from outside Mobile won it. Paul Morphy was a United States chess champion who lived in the 1800s from New Orleans and the award is named for him. He attended Spring Hill College in Mobile, and a street in Fairhope bears his name today.

Spencer graduated, and our team was not as strong for my junior year. I played first board, but lost out on the Morphy and our team finished third in the league behind Theodore and St. Paul, a private school. Clifford Clemon was an able team captain as a senior. I knew we were losing him, but reinforcements were on the way. My younger brother, Paul, was coming to Fairhope the following year and, just as was done for me, I worked him into a B team game as a junior high student. I remember going to sleep the night after a disappointing state tournament not being able to wait for my senior season to begin.

We had a new faculty sponsor for my senior year: Jerry Dixon. Mr. Dixon was a guidance counselor and is very nice man, but he was not a chess coach. In fact, the not so kind inside joke on our team that year was if you could not beat Mr. Dixon, you could not play on the team. The coaching fell to me: who should play whom in practice, what our lineup should be for the next match, etc. It was a distraction to my game, but valuable experience for the future, although I did not yet then know how.

New talent sprang up from the sophomore class: besides Paul there was Tom McCammon, who read anatomy books for fun in his free time, and Tony Caminiti, a free spirit with a natural talent for the game. These three, along with junior Greg Lindley and me made up the varsity team. The talent was pretty evenly spread on our boards 2-5 and as coach, I made sure to work Paul in on second board for at least one match so that we could say we played 1-2 together. Our team ended up with the same record as Theodore and earned a share of Fairhope's first league title. We split possession of the league's perpetual trophy with them over the following year since there was no tie breaking procedure at the time. It was only half of a loaf but we were the first team outside of Mobile to win the league.

As my coaching instinct started to kick in, even then, I looked around for ways to challenge my team and expand the pool of those playing competitive chess. So in the spring of my senior year, I attempted to organize and conduct the first ever Baldwin County Chess Tournament. I wrote letters to the principals of the other county schools. A couple of schools showed interest, but on tournament day only one other showed up: Bayside Academy. The next time they fielded a team is when I took over as coach years later. So even though I didn't coach that squad we played my senior year, I have been involved in every chess match Bayside has ever played!

In preparation for the state tournament, I decided to take the three sophomores with me to Atlanta to play in a Southeast regional tournament there. We stayed at the home of my friend and former teammate, Jack Wiggins, who had moved away when his mother remarried. While there, we ran into Rich Belezza. "Hey Rich," I told him, "we won a share of our first league title this year.

"So, you finally won, huh?" was his replay with a laid-back smile of appreciation. Our team finished third there and Tony won a trophy for top sophomore. I felt that we were ready for state.

Unfortunately, we fell just short, losing to Theodore in the final round and capturing second. I held my opponent to a draw in that match and won an individual trophy for the All-State team. This was at least some consolation for not winning the Morphy. Not winning an outright championship hurt at the time. Still, Fairhope had had its best season ever to date and I could take some satisfaction in knowing that I was leaving the program in better shape than I found it. Theodore was losing much of its senior-heavy team, and the road appeared open for more Fairhope success.

Sure enough, as I went off to college, I heard of Paul's successful exploits during his junior and senior years. In his junior year, Fairhope captured the outright league championship and Tom McCammon won the Morphy. In his senior year, the team was league co-champion and won its first ever State Championship for the school. In addition to all that, Paul was the individual State Champion his junior year and represented Alabama in a tournament of high school champions the following summer. He too served as player/coach, which would also serve him well in the future.

I did not follow the league as closely for the next decade-plus after Paul graduated. The Vigor High Wolves and their "Legion of Doom" dominated the state the year after Paul left, winning the league and state championships. They were coached by James Gipson, who may have been the league's first true chess coach. Then Murphy High School of Mobile, one of the largest public schools in the state, had a string of four league titles in five years.

Baldwin County High School joined the league somewhere along the way, as a growing number of schools from that county finally took up the game. They sneaked in with a league title in the mid-1990s before the rise of the Alabama School of Math and Science (ASMS). This is a public boarding school for grades 10-12 in Mobile that recruits smart students from all over the state. Those students who are accepted pay no tuition since it is funded by the state. As you might expect, they became very good at chess very quickly and won three league championships in the late 1990s.

This decade also saw junior high schools and middle schools join the league and compete. Most notable was the Clark School of Math and Science located at the time in Chickasaw in Mobile County. They assembled a remarkable class of talented eighth graders under the tremendous guidance of Camille Gaston, one of the most generous people you would ever want to meet. Perhaps the most talented of this group was her son, Shaefer, a natural leader. They were so good that they won the league as a middle school in the 1997 season.

The players had to go somewhere for high school in their freshman year, and they could not go to ASMS because that school begins with 10th grade. So, they chose to go to Murphy High. Not surprisingly, this group of freshmen led Murphy to the league title in 1998. Then they all went to ASMS and won the league as sophomores in 1999. Somehow, they stubbed their toes in 2000 and did not win the league their junior year, but all came back for their senior year at ASMS determined to win the league one more time in 2000-2001. That was the season I relocated to Alabama and took the reins at Bayside Academy.

Before I get to that part of the story, I would like to point out two things. First, from 1970, when our league began, until beyond 2000, the league winner almost always went on to win state. If they didn't, it was another team from our league that won. For example, although ASMS won the league title in 1999, Fairhope High crashed the party and took home their second State Championship, coached by the highly intelligent Tim Yahr, a Bayside Academy graduate and strong chess player himself. Mobile was the center of academic chess in the state for over three decades and the state tournament was therefore usually held in Mobile.

Second, it has been a fantastic blessing to have such a large chess league as this in our proverbial back yard, a blessing that is all to easy to take for granted. No league runs without countless hours of thankless work taken on by the league director. Jack Mallory and Lars Britt ran it for many years, some of which when I was a player, and today the tradition is carried on by Jonathan Ling of Daphne High School. Without them, there would be no league.

Relocating and Talking to Bayside

After I graduated high school, I put the game of chess on the shelf. Other than playing in one tournament the year after I finished grad school, I basically did not touch the game for fifteen years. But one great thing about chess is that you can always pick it back up and play it at any point in life! While I clearly enjoyed my time playing chess in high school, I still carried some bitter memories about not having as much success as I would have liked.

Looking back, I now see that part of those negative feelings stemmed from my misunderstanding of the game. As a scholastic player, I played a plodding, defensive, grind it out style of play that was a relief when you won, but excruciating when you lost. Sometimes my mentality veered toward playing not to lose, and that style did not lend itself to fun. Yet that was the only way I knew how to play the game then. I had much to learn. Still, I loved the camaraderie of playing the game with others and thinking strategically, so deep down I knew the game would always be part of me.

After grad school, my career had taken me into the publishing industry in Boston, Massachusetts. I worked there for seven years, after which I had opportunity to relocate to my Alabama home and work for my older brother, Terry, an investment adviser with Southern Capital Services in Daphne. This brought the added bonus of being close to my parents again, and fortunately my New England wife agreed to accompany me to the sunny South!

We arrived in August of 2000 and before my first day on the job I rediscovered that the Mobile-Baldwin Chess League was

14

still going. I knew that Terry's two sons, my nephews Mark and Chris, were entering 10th and 8th grades respectively at Bayside Academy. I wondered: did Bayside want to field a chess team and would my nephews like to play and continue the family tradition?

I placed a call to the school and spoke to Dick Cleveland, the Assistant Headmaster, who I later learned to describe as Bayside's Chief Cook and Bottle Washer. He did everything at the school from arranging schedules to substitutes, and nothing seemed to happen there without him. The school year was just starting so I caught him at a busy time. Our conversation went something like this:

"Mr. Cleveland, this is Eric Nager. Is Bayside interested in having a chess program this year?"

"Well, yes we have a small group of students who are interested in forming a team. I was planning to be the sponsor, but I don't know much about the game and my plate is full."

"I'd be happy to help out with that. I used to play in the local league."

"You want it? You got it!"

With that glorious beginning, I am reminded of the joke in the military that you are never supposed to volunteer for anything. I envisioned myself standing in a formation of people at attention side by side. Then comes the announcement from an unknown, authoritative source, "Whoever wants to be Chess Coach at Bayside Academy, take one step forward!" As I stand there stationary, everyone else in the line to either side of me takes one step backward. "Congratulations, Nager, you have the job!" At least that is what it felt like.I did not mind and I was happy. I had a new opportunity to spend some quality time with my nephews, lead a team, and hopefully have some fun.

What more could any leader want?

Chapter 2

THE FIRST SEASON

My initial expectations as coach were actually pretty low. As mentioned, Bayside at the time was in the 2A athletic classification, one of the smallest in the state. How could we hope to compete against much larger schools with established chess programs? In my mind, if we finished our first season with a .500 record, meaning winning as many matches as we lost, I would have considered that a wildly successful outcome. Having a few laughs along the way with my nephews seemed the most promising potential result.

The First Practice

September rolled around, and I went to the school for our first practice, which had been announced in advance. The outstanding math teacher, Peggy Dyson, had graciously provided her classroom for us to use. Bayside provided me with an official white school golf shirt with the Admiral on it, the school mascot. With that then appropriately attired, I strode into the classroom to meet my new team.

The classroom had desks with metal legs on a hard, linoleum floor. If you turned one desk around to face the one behind it, you could just barely fit a tournament chess board across both slightly inclined surfaces. But one bump or jiggle of the board would send pieces on the edge crashing to the floor, and that year I heard the sound of many tinkling pieces. Having enough room for a chess clock next to the board or a note pad in order for the player to write down his moves was out of the question.

About ten students sat in the classroom waiting for me. Most of them were high schoolers, with a couple of middle schoolers and no elementary kids. Before playing chess to assess their games, I wanted to introduce myself and set down some guidelines for the team. While well intentioned, I see now that how I did it was an example of what not to do as a coach in that situation: I laid down the law before giving myself a chance to get to know them.

"Team, I am Coach Nager. It is good to be here. We are going to have a chess team this year, and there are a few things we need to do to get ready. We WILL practice here every week on Thursday. The season starts soon, and we do not have much time to get ready. We WILL use chess clocks and we WILL notate all of our moves."

I delivered my remarks in a nice way, but it was clearly not what the students wanted to hear. Who wants to be lectured by someone you never met? Reading body language told me that my message was not hitting the mark: uncomfortable shifting in their seats and frowns of disapproval. It was as if they were telling me, "Coach, we just want to play!" Looking back, I'm glad they all did not get up and walk out of the room, never to return!

Fortunately, I recovered quickly enough to let them start

playing and I made a surprising discovery: there was some chess talent in the room! They were led by senior Todd Gardner, who had agitated for starting a team to begin with. I now refer to him as the Godfather of Bayside Chess. Todd had spent one year of high school at the Alabama School of Math and Science, and had a peek behind the curtain at their juggernaut. He had learned how to play against excellent competition and had good experience under his belt, yet he was not the best player on that team. I'm sorry that I only got to coach him for one year.

The distinction of best player fell to sophomore Ryan Willis who had a 1500+ competitive rating. A player's rating is calculated as part of his membership in the United States Chess Federation (USCF). When he plays in sanctioned tournaments, the player's rating rises or falls depending on the results against the strength of his opponents. If we lived somewhere like New York City or California, a 1500 rating for a scholastic player would be unremarkable if not pedestrian. But in southern Alabama, it made him the highest rated player in our league by a wide margin. In fact, in 16 years of coaching I have only coached one player with a higher rating than Ryan's.

We also had seniors Michael Buder and Justine Brent, juniors Brian Wolf and Billy Roden, and sophomores Mark Nager and Matt Norman. Rounding out the team were 8th grader Chris Nager, and 7th grader David Gardner, Todd's brother. This gave us just enough to fill out an A team and a B team with five players each.

Of course, all of our players were not at practice every week for one reason or another. Right next to Mrs. Dyson's room was the classroom used as the detention hall for students who got in trouble during the day. They had detention from 3:00-4:00, which overlapped with the first portion of our practice time. I remember looking through the window and scowling at Chris one week as he had committed some minor infraction that landed him in detention. His response was smiling at me and waving.

The First Scrimmage

In light of the talent we had, I began to be optimistic about our chances for the season. Maybe we could win more matches than we lost and eke out a winning record. I was forgetting that outside of Todd and Ryan, no one on the team had played competitive chess before in any serious way. I was a rookie coach and did not yet know how to develop raw talent. Yes, they were intelligent students and fast learners, but the first match was less than a month away.

I looked around for someone we could play against to simulate match conditions, and I finally found my answer about two blocks away from Bayside Academy: Christ the King School. Christ the King is a Catholic school incorporating grades K-8 and had been in the chess league for several years. I reached out to their coach, Ed Rutkowski, who was more than happy to accommodate us. They practiced on Thursday afternoon, just as we did in order to line up with the days in which league matches were played. So I grabbed my team and we trooped up the road to their school.

This match will be a good measuring stick for us, I thought. My team of high school kids ought to be able to handle a team of middle school kids, even if they are more experienced. In general, high school students have longer attention spans and more patience than middle schoolers. In a timed chess match between the two, the older students usually win because the younger ones tend to make the first mistakes.

I set my lineup with Ryan and Todd at the top two boards and we began to play. The result deflated me: Christ the King 4, Bayside 1. Ryan had won his game, but we were swept on boards 2-5. If we just got trounced by a middle school, this was going to be a long season! Little did I know that this was no ordinary middle school.

Christ the King was loaded with talent that year. Led by eighth graders Jay Smith, Sam Davis, J.B. Galle, David Mackey, Logan Chambers, and Matt Allen, they went on to win the middle school division in our league before going on to become junior high State Champions in the spring. Best of all, all of those players with the exception of Logan came to Bayside Academy for high school and formed the nucleus of a powerhouse team over those four years.

In the immediate aftermath of that loss, though, I was left to wonder if we really had a chance to win any matches that season. We headed back down to Bayside with our figurative tails tucked between our legs to take stock of the situation. But we did not have much time to think about it. By the time I was able to arrange the exhibition match, it was only a week before our first league match. We were heading into battle again soon, only this time it was going to count. We were as ready as we were ever going to be.

The First Match

The next week we drove across Mobile Bay to Mobile for our match, only to find out we were playing the public high school from our own city: Daphne. Usually for the first match of the season, the tournament director does not know for sure which teams are coming until they show up at the playing hall. Only then does he pair the first round, so you find out who you play when you get there.

Sometimes the league is played in a round robin format, such that each team plays each of the others in their division. In that case the schedule can be published in advance, or at least after the first round. If there are many teams, I have seen the league paired in what is known as a Swiss system, which is how most chess tournaments are done. In this case, teams that win in the first round are paired against each other in the second, and teams that lose in the first round are paired against other first round losers. The goal is to yield a clear winner by the end of the season. But you still have to wait until the end of each round to see how the standings look. The larger point is that unlike athletic leagues, it is not unusual in chess not to know who you are playing in advance.

In those years our league featured five-player teams, and there was an A, B, and C league. The pairings were done at the A team level with the lower divisions following, so any two given schools whose A teams played each other also faced off for B and C teams. Sometimes a school would only field an A team and in that case, the opposing school's B and C teams won by forfeit. (We have since modified the rules so that B and C teams compete together in their own JV league, independent from the A teams.)

Time was also a factor. Then we played one match per month with a time control of game in 60 minutes (G/60). If you have never seen a chess clock, it has two faces on it – one for each player. While a player is thinking about his move, his clock is running. When he makes a move he touches his clock, stopping it from running and activating his opponent's side to run. The game continues until one player loses or runs out of time. In a G/60 scenario, it means that each player has 60 minutes on his clock and if both players use the maximum amount of time, the game can last no longer than two hours.

As a coach, I cannot talk to my players during a match. Our league etiquette dictates that the coach stand behind his players when observing a match so he cannot make eye contact with his team and intentionally or unintentionally signal them. I cannot call timeout or yell, "What are you doing?" when I see a bad move. Coaching chess is definitely not for control freaks because once the match starts, you are totally powerless.

Our first opponent, Daphne High, was a 6A school. They had many more students than Bayside and were an athletic powerhouse, especially in football. They also had an experienced chess team, mostly of juniors, with whom we would tangle repeatedly over my first couple of years. Based on our scrimmage results, we were decided underdogs in my mind. Yet as you will see, our story is one of continual surprise and our first match was no exception. The final score was Bayside 4, Daphne 1.

Scoring the first league wins in Bayside history were Ryan Willis, Todd Gardner, Brian Wolf, and Justine Brent and the team win set the tone for a very successful inaugural campaign.

The next month we took on Fairhope High, another 6A school and my alma mater, the team I least wanted to play. They were shorthanded and had to forfeit a couple of the lower boards, and we prevailed 4-1. After 15 years, Bayside had avenged the loss from the county tournament my senior year in high school!

Next we took on and defeated B.C. Rain, a 5A high school from Mobile, again by a 4-1 count. The calendar flipped to January of 2001 and we took on a school more our size: Clark School of Math & Science, a middle school and the overall defending league champs. While their great players who had won league and state championships had graduated, their players still received good instruction and they definitely knew what to do with the pieces. We squeaked out a hard fought 3-2 victory and there were suddenly only two undefeated teams left in the league: Bayside and the Alabama School of Math & Science, our next opponent.

To be playing for a league championship in our first year was way beyond my best expectations. But now we were running up against a group of players who, from grades 8-11, had won three league championships and three State Championships in four years. As the match began, I had a flicker of hope as ASMS had not yet shown up and we were allowed to start our opponent's clocks. But they soon arrived and proceeded to take us apart by a score of 4-1. While we have not lost many matches during my tenure at Bayside, I have never been as proud of a team in defeat as I was of that one. All the players took their time and fought hard. There is no shame in losing to a better team. That year ASMS swept the A, B, and C league titles.

On the individual side, Ryan won his game on first board

and took home the Morphy Award as league's best player with a perfect 6-0 score. I later told him that it felt as if I had won the award that eluded me as a player. A few years later when I became a parent, I realized that for me it is more fun to watch my children enjoy an activity than it is for me to experience it myself, and there is an element of that in coaching as well.

In our first year in the league, Bayside Academy burst on the scene and took outright second place with a 5-1 record. But there was more to come. My high school dream was finally realized as by then, Baldwin County hosted an annual one-day chess tournament and Bayside was happy to join in the fun. We played seven matches that day with about a G/20 time control. On the one hand we were able to avenge our defeat to Christ the King in the scrimmage match with a decisive 4-1 win. On the other, we fell to Daphne High in our rematch with them, and they went on to win the event.

Next up was the state tournament at local Fairhope High. ASMS still loomed there as the team to beat, but we were having our own problems with the other opponents. In the first round we drew, or tied, UMS-Wright. In the second we drew Murphy High, and in the third we faced the ASMS B team. In this event we played four-player teams, which makes ties more common but does not give either team a color advantage. (In chess it is considered a very slight advantage to be white since you get to move first.)

Ryan won his game and Todd and Matt Norman lost theirs, leaving it up to my nephew Mark on third board. However, when I looked at his game he was WAY behind. One aspect of chess that makes it a good tool for learning math is that all the pieces have numeric values. Pawns are considered worth one point each, knights and bishops are worth three, rooks are worth five, and a queen is worth ten. As a coach who walks around looking at many games being played simultaneously, I can tell at a glance if my player is winning or losing by the value of the pieces left on the board, or captured on the side of the board.

In this case Mark was down by a rook and a pawn or two, a hole out of which most players should not be able to climb. Since his was the last game going, I sat down behind him and mentally went through an end of season condolence speech to the team. "Well guys," it went in my head, "we had a really good year. You should be proud. Let's work hard and come back strong next year." Or something like that. My head was down despondently as I was thinking these thoughts, but when I looked up something strange was happening. Mark's opponent was in severe time trouble, and Mark had worked a pawn down almost to the other side of the board.

Mark was able to turn the tables and pull out an improbable victory, giving Bayside our third drawn match of the day. At the end of the game, Todd Gardner gave Mark a big bear hug in relief that his senior year would be extended for one more match and that he'd have a chance to redeem himself from his third-round loss. This was because the teams we had drawn were also drawing each other so that after three rounds there was a four-way tie for second. The ASMS A team was declared the clear winner at that point, and those seniors deservedly went out on top.

Meanwhile, the four teams in second place were paired against each other for one final round in an attempt to break the tie. We were paired again against UMS and this time dispatched them 3-1. Murphy and ASMS B drew, so Bayside emerged as clear second in our first state tournament. It was quite a first year. As Mark's game illustrated, you should never give up.

You never know what might happen.

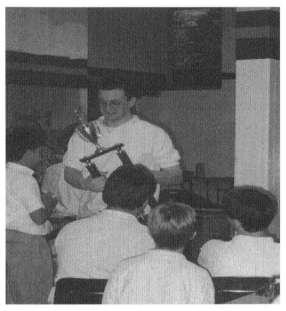

Bayside's first chess trophy being clutched by Senior Captain Todd Gardner in our first season, 2001. We have since won over 100 as a team, more than half of which are first place trophies.

Chapter 3

THE SECOND SEASON AND VENTURING OUT

Double State Champions

The second school year opened with an incredible influx of chess talent to Bayside. While we lost Todd, Michael, and Justine to graduation, that was more than made up by the skill pouring in from Christ the King. Jay Smith and Sam Davis immediately stepped into varsity team roles as freshmen. Another pleasant surprise was the arrival of an incredibly intelligent 6th grader named Landon Sykora, who also qualified for the varsity in his first match.

This year we had moved to the library for our practice site instead of Mrs. Dyson's room. I remember meeting with the team and talking to them about goals and expectations for the year. It was then I learned the opposite natures of Jay and Sam. Jay was establishment – the obedient follower of rules, and it is no surprise he went on to serve his country in the military after attending the Merchant Marine Academy. Sam was the rebel.

Before my opening speech to the team, I overheard them talking to each other. Sam started with bragging, "I'm going to play first board and win all of my games, dominate everyone."

29

Jay listened patiently. "Where are you going to play, Jay?"

Without hesitation he answered, "Wherever Coach tells me to." While both players contributed to the program tremendously over the years and both types are indispensable for success, from a coach's standpoint, your face lights up when you hear an unsolicited response like Jay's!

Having learned lessons from season one, my opening speech went something like this, "We had a great season last year, and almost won league, county and state. We have more and better players now, so I think with some effort we can win all three. This is our goal. It will take hard work on your part, but I am here to help you. Come to practice, apply yourselves, and you will have a spot on this team."

I was aware that most of my chess players also played varsity sports for the school and sometimes there were conflicts with practices and matches. I told the team, "If you have a game with a sports team on a day when we have practice, do not worry about it and play the game. You are still representing Bayside." I knew this was not always reciprocated to us because sometimes my players would be punished if they missed a sports practice for a chess match. I wanted the players to know, "I am here for you. You are not here for me." I have yet to hear of one my players going on to play professional sports.

The season started off even stronger than the first one. We swept St. Dominic's 5-0 in the season opener and then blasted McGill-Toolen 4-1. The December match featured a showdown with city rival Daphne and I liked our chances. That year they were a team made up mostly of experienced seniors, compared to our younger team, and unknown to me was that Daphne also had some Christ the King graduates who had been teammates with some of our guys. I realized after the fact that some of our players were a little intimidated by that relationship.

Jay and Sam drew their matches on boards three and four, while Mark won on two and Landon lost on five. Shockingly, Ryan Willis, who had gone 19-1 for Bayside so far in his career, lost on first board to senior Amin Tavana and we lost the match. Our hopes for a league title were severely dimmed, and even more painful, Ryan quit the team. Not only did we lose the match, but the best player in the league! Now the season was scrambled.

I should add here that my shortcomings as a coach added to the woes. Before the first match, I put together a list of "fineable" offenses and handed them out to the team. It was an effort to educate the players in humorous way, but it did not go over as intended. For example, a player might be fined fifty cents if he lost a game after being ahead materially by a knight or bishop. I never intended to collect. Instead, I wanted my players to think.

However, these were not professional baseball players who missed a sign from the third base coach. A couple of players circulated the list around campus as a joke, and therefore the team did not take it seriously. Worse, I left off a very important item: the one time a player *can* talk to his coach during a match is if his opponent offers him a draw. This is only in the presence of a tournament director and the coach can only respond by saying something like a draw will help us (take it), or a draw will not help us (decline it).

In the Daphne match, Jay was offered a draw by his opponent, and he promptly accepted, probably because he was playing an older opponent and he thought that was the best he could do. But if he had asked me, I would have told him to play on because of the team situation. At best, had this been done, it only would have have given us the possibility of a tie instead of a loss, but it was still a gross oversight on my part. It would be another ten years of coaching before that situation arose again at a critical time.

The immediate concern was putting together a first board by committee. I played my nephew Mark, then a junior, on first board for the next two matches. He split those games, and the team won both, putting us back in contention for the league because ASMS had defeated Daphne. So a final round clash loomed against our nemesis. If we could defeat them, we would win a share of the league title.

But a funny quirk in the schedule that year placed the state tournament before our final round league match. That, combined with the fact that the senior leadership at ASMS that had graduated the year before combined to throw a logistical hurdle in their path such that they were unable to attend. Earlier I mentioned Camille Gaston. Her generosity toward chess teams extended well beyond her own, and her standing offer at the time was to sponsor our league champion in the state tournament.

Without a league champion decided yet though, there was no team to sponsor. ASMS had won the league so many times, they apparently relied on this method of funding and when it was not available, they were unable to make the trip. There would be a new State Champion for 2002. I did not know this until we arrived at the tournament and saw to my amazement that they were not there.

For our part, I dutifully loaded eight players on the school bus and drove four hours to the southern outskirts of Birmingham, Alabama's largest city. No parents accompanied us, so I was responsible for the whole lot. After making sure each was in his hotel room for the night, I assigned Mark as my roommate and turned in.

While not yet a parent, I was awakened in the early morning hours by what I can only describe as paternal instinct. I am not naturally an early riser, so to wake up that early is very unusual for me. When I did, I noticed the power had been out in our room, and therefore probably the entire hotel: our alarm clocks would not go off at the right time in the morning. So I stayed up the next couple of hours until it was time to wake the team, made sure they ate a good breakfast, and drove them to the tournament venue.

When I noticed on the registration sheet that we were the only team from southern Alabama, I probably had an expression on my face like the cat who swallowed the canary. That still did not mean we had easy competition. To the contrary, the two top teams in northern Alabama, who had battled it out for the championship of their small league, were there: Hoover High and John Carroll. For those who remember the ESPN special from the mid-2000s on Hoover, they were a perennial national power in high school football, winning multiple 6A championships and boasting the largest school in the state. John Carroll, who had defeated Hoover that season, was a 5A private school with tremendous resources at their disposal.

In the opening round we played a team from Fayette, a newcomer to chess. The tournament director was a stickler and let no coaches in the room, so I was forced to watch from a tiny window in the door of a classroom that functioned as the playing hall. I tried to protest. "Sir, I know the proper etiquette of a chess coach and coaches are present in our league matches."

"I'm sorry." he said. "My policy is that no coaches or parents may come in the room."

"Parents I understand." I sympathized. "But coaches are required to know the rules."

"You are going to have to be outside the room like everyone else." He won no points for customer service, but tournament directors do have ultimate authority to decide these things.

Since I could not see much, I decided to put some excess equipment back in the bus. No sooner was I walking back from the parking lot than an excited Sam Davis ran out to meet me, declaring, "Coach, I won my game!" We were off to a good start and finished off pasting Fayette 4-0.

The State Tournament in Alabama is a rated event of four-player teams, and the team must play in rating, or strength order. My lineup for the event were freshmen Sam and Jay on the top two boards, Mark Nager on third, and senior Brian Wolf on fourth. In the second round we took on Hoover and drubbed them by the same 4-0 count. In the junior high division, things were going equally well as our team won their first two matches also led by David Gardner, Chris Nager, David Mackey and James Adams.

In the final round, the varsity team faced John Carroll while the junior high took on the Alabama School of Fine Arts(ASFA). This was a similar school to ASMS, but with a different focus, located in the northern part of the state, and at the junior high level. We battled ASFA to a 2-2 draw, but because they had a blemish on their record earlier in the day, we were Junior High State Champions. Not long after that, we became High School State Champions, as we defeated John Carroll 2-0-2, with Sam and Jay drawing on the top boards. In our second year of existence as a program, we took an outright double State Championship.

To say I was elated was an understatement. We ate a celebratory dinner at Waffle House on the way home, and I remember thinking, no doubt with a big grin on my face, that I had accomplished everything that could be done as a scholastic chess coach in Alabama. Not only was I dead wrong about that, but we were soon to be brought back down to earth later that month. The best analogy is that of the conquering Roman generals when they came home to parades in their honor. Standing behind them in their chariots were slaves whose job it was to whisper in their ears as the adoring crowds cheered them that all glory is fleeting.

After being home a few days, we had to play ASMS on their campus to determine our league champion. They had heard of our success at state, and no doubt begrudged us taking a title they felt was theirs. Since Sam had played so well on first board at state, I played him there against ASMS and he managed a draw against the kid who won the Morphy that year. The rest of the team did not fare as well, with only Brian getting a victory on board three. We lost the match and took third in the league.

Some might say we did not deserve to win state that year because we were not even the best team in our own league. While the latter part of that statement is true, a big part of success in life is showing up, and we had superior logistics to our competitors. And, even in events when all possible teams are competing, the best one doesn't always win. In fairness had Ryan stayed with the team, I think we would have at least tied ASMS and shown we were their equal. As it was, the season was a split decision, and a wildly successful one at that from my perspective.

Montreal

Chess season is pretty intense for me, so after it is over, I like to relax and get away from the game. In the summer of 2002, my wife and I vacationed in Montreal, Canada. We went to a comedy festival. We rented bikes and rode around the beautiful city. We ate good food. One day we were walking along and I saw a sign for a store that had a chess symbol on it. I had to stop there!

I began speaking with the proprietor, Larry Bevand, who I soon learned was the head of scholastic chess in the nation of Canada where the subject is taught as a math course in fifth grade nationwide. Incidentally, Canada has higher standardized test scores in math than the U.S. His shop was a retail outlet for chess sets, clocks and boards, but it was also a wholesale supplier to chess organizations around the world. I toured his store, which had an upstairs playing area for tournaments, and ordered a display board for teaching my team.

Then the light bulb came on. I asked, "So Larry, do your teams travel other places to play?"

"Oh yeah, all the time."

"Would you be interested in visiting Alabama during the

Canadian winter? It's much warmer down there!"

"That's true."

"Your players could stay with host families and attend classes with my team. They could probably even teach the French class! Also, we have Mardi Gras down there."

"What are the ratings of your players?"

"Most are 1,000 and below."

"I'm sorry, that is too low to be competitive with my players."

"Well why don't you send younger players with lower ratings then to make it a fair fight?"

"That would not be fair to the older players who have earned the right to travel."

The man was determined not to have a creative thought about helping to make this idea work. Still, the trip and the conversation helped me develop a sense of vision for the team and I filed away the idea of international travel for future reference.

Going to Biloxi

The one constant in coaching is player turnover. Gone to graduation and Rice University was Brian Wolf, who had turned in a perfect 10-0 record for his senior season. I expected to lose him. Also gone from the State Championship team was first board Sam Davis, who unexpectedly chose not to play for his sophomore or junior seasons. Fortunately, the returning players were improving.

One key to getting better is playing stronger, outside competition. In the fall of 2002, I discovered the perfect opportunity in the form of a tournament held in Biloxi, Mississippi. Biloxi is about half way between Daphne and New Orleans along the Gulf Coast, and is perhaps best known for their casinos. Jean Troendle, who at that time ran an organization called Cajun Chess, held regular tournaments there for adult and scholastic players. The attraction to this for us was that these events drew a significant number of players from the strong scholastic chess league in New Orleans who would help serve as a good measuring stick for our program. How would we stack up against them?

We were about to find out as I took five players to the President's Casino. One nice thing about the casinos there is that most of them offer a pretty good all you can eat buffet at a reasonable price. This is probably at best a break-even proposition for them as they attempt to lure more people there for the gaming side of their business. But we were not there to gamble. The plan was to enjoy a good meal together as a team after the tournament before heading back home, and the parents seemed to like this idea.

Again, the results turned out better than expected. Each player played five games, for a total of 25. Of those, Bayside won fourteen, lost nine, and tied two. It was an individual as well as a team event, with the top three scores counting as the team score. Our top three scorers did well enough to qualify for a first place trophy in the K-12 division. So we brought home to Bayside the lofty title of World Amateur Champions, since that was the name of the tournament. I have no idea how widely advertised it was around the world.

The following year, although our individual players did not score as well, we still captured first as a team. That year we were the Gulf Coast Amateur Champions. In the spring of 2005 we won again, but by then the event was downgraded to merely the Gulf Coast Open. Nevertheless, these events showed our potential to be successful outside of Alabama against good competition. In August of 2005, Hurricane Katrina blew through New Orleans and Biloxi, and these tournaments went on hiatus.

We gladly took the opportunities when they were available and tried to apply them to our league. In the case of our third season, it was with mixed results. For the first time in the 2002-2003 season, our league went to four-player teams to parallel the state tournament. When our program began, Bayside, as a smaller school, would have benefited from a four-player team since we did not have as much depth as other larger teams then. But as we grew in talent and depth, the shift to four-player teams probably hurt us.

At no time was that shift more evident than when we took on St. Dominic's. We had started the season 3-0, but ran into the team that went on to win the junior high State Championship that year. They were talented, and they held us to a 2-2 draw. This put enormous pressure on us the following match when we played ASMS because we had to beat them to get ahead of them in the standings. A 2-2 tie would keep ASMS in first place.

The good news was that this showdown match would be held at Bayside for the first time. Finally, the student body would get to see us play. Word had gotten around the school that we were good and winning, but the athletes in particular made fun of the chess players. Never mind that almost all of the chess team played some kind of sport. That year it was soccer, and when our players had to leave soccer practice early for a chess match, they would get razzed.

In some scholastic chess leagues around the country, matches are set with designated home and away teams. At our monthly league matches, the entire league shows up and plays in one place. So it was good for our school athletes to come by and see 150 raucous kids having a blast playing chess. Unlike what you might think, it is loud in there! Seeing this changed their perception of chess and the razzing stopped.

That was an important victory for our program, but it did not help us win the match at hand. And right beforehand I was presented with a dilemma. Ryan Willis showed up and wanted to play. He did not deserve to because he had not practiced with the team and had left us in the lurch the year before. But he seemed repentant and wanted to help us beat ASMS, so I gave in. In the end it did not matter.

The first year ASMS beat us 4-1. The second year it was 3-1-1. This time it was 2-1-1, so while we were narrowing the gap and lost by the narrowest of margins, it did not make the loss or finishing second in our league any less excruciating. To make matters worse, we were shorthanded for the state tournament because of a competing soccer event. The tournament was after our league, so ASMS was fully funded and present. They beat us again there en route to the State Championship and we settled for second, as did our junior high team.

Knowing we were facing a difficult task, I toyed with the idea of putting our better middle school players on the junior high team and attempting to win at least one state title. But Jay Smith, who was quickly becoming a team leader and who had skipped the soccer event to play chess, bluntly disabused me of that idea. "Jay, if we play Landon on the junior high team, we can maybe win that division and walk out of here with a State Championship."

"Coach, there is no way we are coming up here and not giving it our best shot." It was a point well taken, and I placed 7th grader Landon Sykora on the varsity team where he belonged.

Landon had come a long way in being respected by his peers for his strong play. As a little sixth grader the year before, he annoyed some of the older players by asking, "Are we there yet?" soon after the bus had left the parking lot to a match. But in fairness, in those early years we were mostly a high school team, and younger players were the exception.

The only bright spot that season was capturing our first Baldwin County Tournament title. We beat two-time defending champ Daphne and ended with the same record as Fairhope. To break the tie we played a team speed game, where instead of the normal 30 minutes per side, each player had five. I do not like to have my players play speed in practice because I think it tends to make them play faster, but it is a good exercise to help you think fast under pressure. Despite our inexperience with the format, we prevailed. Our best performances still lay ahead of us.

Double State Champions Again

Before the season began, I made one of my smartest moves as a coach. At the suggestion of brother Terry, I appointed the first newly created position of Team Mom/Dad. Valerie Smith, Jay's mom, was the logical choice. "Val, I'd like you to be our Team Mom."

"What would be my duties?" she asked nervously.

"Well, we have one match a month in our league. The main job would be to coordinate transportation and snacks for each match and help arrange the team party at the end of the year." I had figured out by then that we played much worse on an empty stomach.

"I guess I can do that."

"Congratulations!" I exclaimed. It was kind of like how I became chess coach, except that she did not volunteer. We developed a good relationship, and as time went on, I came up with more ideas for the team, some of which expanded the duties of Team Mom. It got to the point where I'd say, "Hey Val, I've got a great idea!"

"Oh no."

The term of Team Mom is only for one year at a time, and we do rotate the position.

Season four opened with a disappointing tie against Daphne. The last thing I wanted was to face ASMS again with a blemish on our record. However, our team had improved. While Mark

Nager graduated, I landed my first successful recruit at Bayside: J.B. Galle. J.B. was one of the Christ the King kids, but he had gone to Daphne High for his freshman and sophomore years. Now he wanted to come to Bayside and play chess with his friends, and we were delighted to have him.

Before I move on to the 2003-2004, a few more words about Mark are in order. It could not have been easy playing for me as my nephew and he was a natural leader on the team. One time I was caught in traffic on the way to the match and when I got there, play had already begun. Mark set the lineup just as I would have done. He was also a smooth talker. Another time, we were leaving the Bayside parking lot on the bus heading for a match, and I saw out the window a cop had pulled Mark over for speeding. I crossed him off my lineup for that match and learned later that he had talked his way out of a ticket.

Also new on the team that year were Stephen Smith, Jay's brother, and Joey Nickerson, both freshmen. These two had insatiable chess appetites, especially Stephen, and any open surface around them soon became occupied with a chess board. Actually, Stephen didn't even need a board. I remember riding with him to the state tournament and playing a game of chess in our heads, where we would call out our moves and have to envision the position on the board. The first player to make an illegal move lost, and Stephen was able to play for twenty moves without a mistake, a Bayside record that still stands today.

This talent gave me the tremendous luxury of loading up the junior high team with Landon, Stephen, and Joey, along with Matthew Wolf, brother of Brian, and it paid off as they tied ASMS 2-2 in the December match. The long ASMS winning streak stretching back over three years was broken, and now our varsity team stood again on level ground with them. Thus softened up by our junior high, the varsity defeated ASMS in January by a 3-1 count. Not only was it our first victory over them, it gave us our first outright league championship.

Winning the league was especially sweet to me because I had been chasing it so long as both a player and a coach. Just as impressive, our junior high team finished second overall, ahead of all the other high school teams. It was the first and only time that two different teams from the same school finished 1-2 in the league.

We successfully defended our county title and then it was on to state. The varsity team of Jay, J.B., David Gardner, and Chris Nager was a formidable group, and the championship came down to battling John Carroll again, the best team from north Alabama. Bayside prevailed 3-1. At the junior high level, it bordered on not being fair as we took the title over Shades Mountain.

After the championship we drove home to Daphne and arrived at Bayside Saturday night. There was a dance in the gym and my players wanted to attend. I escorted them to the door where we were met by Grant Blackburn, a student, who was friends with Chris.

"How'd you all do?" he asked.

"We won state," Chris replied in his understated manner.

"Y'all are the best chess team in the world!" exalted Grant as he embraced Chris in a bear hug.

This time winning state was not a fluke. We were league champions and had taken on and defeated the best teams in the state. In our first four years we had dominated at the local, state, and regional levels. It was time to consider stepping onto the national stage,

Winning a regional event. Before we went to our first nationals, we won some regional tournaments in nearby Biloxi, Mississippi. Here we are after one of them. Left to Right: Assistant Coach Kevin Spriggs, Jay Smith, J.B. Galle, Chris Nager, David Mackey, Coach Eric Nager.

Double State Champions. In our second season we won the Alabama Team High School and Middle School State Chess Championships in Pelham, Alabama. L-R: James Adams, David Gardner, Sam Davis, Chris Nager, Brian Wolf, Coach Eric Nager, David Mackey, Jay Smith, and Mark Nager.

Chapter 4

PREPARING FOR SUPER NATIONALS III, NASHVILLE, 2005

Super Nationals II, Kansas City, 2001

Every spring the U.S. Chess Federation (USCF) conducts a high school, junior high, and elementary school Nationals. In most years, these are three separate events taking place in different cities at different times. Every fourth year though, all three events come together into one location and time and this is known as Super Nationals.

The start of my fifth year of coaching, the 2004-2005 academic year, was the year we considered going to our first Nationals, and that so happened to be a Super Nationals year. The location of Nashville was appealing, because it was so close. From Daphne, it is about an eight-hour drive and it is in the Central Time Zone, as we are.

Fortunately, some of my players actually had some experience at a Super Nationals, having attended the one in Kansas City in 2001 as eighth graders from Christ the King. Matt Allen's mom, Beverly, had saved programs, records, and materials from the event that she kept in a manilla envelope and handed it all over to me at the beginning of the season. I eagerly asked her about it. "Was there a viewing area to watch the games?"

"At the hotel we stayed, there was a viewing platform, but it was far away from the games. If the player you wanted to see was on the other side of the playing area, you couldn't see anything."

"What was the coolest part?"

"I liked the opening ceremony." she enthused. "There was a parade of State Champions in alphabetical order. Because Christ the King was Junior High State Champion for Alabama that year, we led the parade" (because Alabama comes first alphabetically). "In front of us was (International Master) Josh Waitzkin, and the kids got to meet him." I knew that Waitzkin was the subject of the movie *Searching for Bobby Fischer,* a popular and true story about chess. All of this sounded wonderfully fun and interesting, and made me want our team to experience it all. But first we had a season to play.

The Perfect Season

Another great aspect of our dominating performance the previous season was that we had no seniors, and therefore no losses to graduation. Everyone was coming back with one notable exception: Landon Sykora transferred to another school. It is one thing to lose a player like Ryan who stayed at Bayside. It is another to lose a player of Landon's caliber, and then have to play against him when he is on another team. Unfortunately, the players we have lost to other schools over the years could make up their own all-star team.

Landon was the first, and although we did not feel his loss immediately because of all the returning talent, players like him do not come along every day. His three-year record at Bayside as a 6th-8th grader, playing mostly on the varsity level, was 38-6-5, including a Junior High State Championship. At the time of his departure, that was the second most wins of any player I had coached to that point. I will always remember his insight as he shared his process for thinking though what would make a good gift for me at one of our season ending team parties, "I don't think Coach Nager is the Home Depot kind of guy." Of course not! I'm a chess coach.

Landon's loss was partially offset by the return of Sam Davis for his senior year. I guess Sam had heard how much fun his friends on the soccer team were having playing chess and he wanted back in on the action. Sadly, for him, I had no place to play him on the varsity team at the beginning of the year. I should add that after all of our success, it was now *very* cool to play chess at Bayside Academy. Jay Smith played first board for us that year, and I remember his girlfriend coming to all the matches to sit and watch him play. We had our own groupies!

We were so deep that year, that the second-best team in the league by far was our own B team. When the first match rolled around, I held out of competition a team of four players because I had nowhere to play them. That team was J.B. Galle, Sam Davis, Chris Nager, and David Mackey. All four had been part of a State Championship team for us in the past and Chris had been a member of two. That year, we ceased competing against other teams and were instead only competing against ourselves.

The one thing those four players had in common was that they were all seniors. If possible, I prefer to rely on younger players because I have more time with them, and sophomores Stephen Smith and Joey Nickerson were ready to step into boards two and three on the varsity team. Junior David Gardner was the fourth. It is difficult to describe how good it felt as a coach to be leading a team like this. I felt as if I had harnessed a tiger and that no other team could mess with us. Only later would I learn how quickly such a good thing can fall apart, but also how quickly it can be built back again.

The varsity team rolled through the regular season with a perfect 4-0 score in each of our six league matches, a combined 24-0-0 for the year. This undefeated, untied, and unscored upon mark was the first and only perfect season turned in at the varsity level in league history that I am aware and a great way to defend our first title from the previous year. Jay Smith captured the second Morphy Award in Bayside history, but that was not all.

The B and C teams marched through the season undefeated also. The C team duplicated the A team's feat of a perfect 24-0, and the B team stumbled only once: in the January match they were held to a 2-2 draw by McGill-Toolen. Each of those teams finished tied for first in their divisions only because they did not face the teams with which they had the same record. Ironically, both of our teams lost the tiebreaker on paper and had to settle for the second-place trophies. Still, a combined team mark for the season of 70-2-0 is not bad.

Next came the county tournament. I was away attending the birth of my daughter, but I spoke to Joey's dad, Nick, on the phone and got a blow by blow report. I do not remember much of this conversation because I was so excited about being a dad, but again the varsity crushed all opposition, this time in a five-player format, by perfect 5-0 scores against Christ the King, Daphne, Fairhope, and Spanish Fort en route to our third consecutive county title. This left the combined varsity record at an eye-popping 44-0-0 for the year.

Another quirk of scheduling left the state tournament after Nationals that year. The Nationals story is the subject of another chapter, so I will just relate the state portion here. We drove to the campus of Samford University off of beautiful Lakeshore Drive in southern Birmingham to defend our title and try to win our third State Championships in our first five years as a program. We were a little short handed for that event, without the services of David Gardner and J.B. Galle, but with such depth it was effortless to plug in Sam Davis at fourth board who had played first board for us as a freshman. I also entered a B team in the varsity section, including Chris who would attend Samford the following year.

In the first round the domination continued, as we blasted Randolph High of Huntsville 4-0. But then the tournament director matched us against our own B team in the second round. In a situation like this, to avoid potential conflicts of interest, chess protocol really calls for not scheduling two teams from the same school against each other unless there was no other possible match up, and that early in the tournament, there were other options. I protested to the same tournament director who handled the tournament two years ago: "Why are we playing our own team in the second round?"

"Do you object?" he asked callously.

"Yes, I object! We did not drive 250 miles to play ourselves.

We can do that in practice."

"The pairing stands." I thought I kept my composure, but the dad of one player later said that was the maddest he ever saw me get.

My real concern lay in not wanting the B team to damage the A team's chances by possibly drawing them. The players on our team play each other many times in practice during the long course of the season. They know each other's tendencies and weaknesses better than any opponent we play, and the potential for the stronger player to lose is greater. If one player consistently beats his teammate in practice, he might start to take him lightly in a meaningful game, or he might take sympathy on him and not want to beat him badly. All of this has to be put aside in tournament play.

As the coach, it is a helpless feeling watching one of your teams play another. I recognized this dynamic of familiarity was at play and just wanted to get past this round with our A team unscathed. Sure enough on board three, Joey was having a tremendous struggle against his friend, Rico Moorer. At a state tournament every board win counts, so you do not want to drop a game, even if the team wins by a 3-1 count. Joey held on for the win in a tense end game, the A team won 4-0, I breathed a sigh of relief, and we moved on to the third round.

There we returned to our bludgeoning ways by dispatching St. Paul's of Mobile 4-0. St. Paul's was coached by the amiable Kevin Dolbeare, who moved to ASMS the following year. That set up a final round rematch against our old foe at state: John Carroll. Their coach was an enthusiastic fellow, but one I did not completely respect as a chess coach. This is because he instructed his players not to take the required chess notation in the matches, but instead to place check marks for each move on the notation sheet. If he was coaching beginning elementary school children, that would be one thing, but these were high school students fully capable of writing.

I assume the intent of this practice was so that his players would not be distracted by writing down their moves and be able to concentrate better on their games. I thought it was a Mickey Mouse practice, unworthy of such a prestigious school, and was frustrated that the tournament director took little action. As I recall, the only consequence was giving their team five less minutes on their clocks for the game.

We were one match away from a perfect season. John Carroll had been drawn earlier in the tournament, so they had to beat us outright in order to claim the title. Given our record so far that season, that would seem to be a tall order, and indeed it was. Yet, John Carroll not only scored on us that final match, but they earned a 2-2 draw. Maybe our top players were running low on gas after such a long season, but the Smith boys, Jay and Stephen, fell on the top two boards while Joey and Sam saved the day by winning on three and four.

At first it almost felt like a little bit of a letdown, but that feeling did not linger. We were State Champions again and the great group of seniors we had went out on top. In the sense of sweeping all the team events we entered that year, it was a perfect season.

The Logistics Plan

Next, we had to plan for Nationals. We could only do this in a logistical sense because in a chess sense, we could not even simulate game conditions at the big tournament. As mentioned, in our league we played game in 60 at the time, meaning a game could last as long as two hours if both players used all of their time. Our practices were two hours long, so we could simulate one of those games, which we played once per month. The county and state tournaments had even shorter time controls. At Nationals, it was game in 120, meaning each game could last as long as four hours. And it was not just one game, but seven of them played over a three-day period.

Even though a couple of our players had experienced this four years earlier, I decided that all of them would have to sink or swim when we got there and to focus my efforts on getting the team there. The tournament ran from 1:00 Friday afternoon to 6:00 Sunday afternoon. I wanted to try and keep expenses down, which meant minimizing the number of hotel nights, and I wanted the students to miss as little school as possible for the sake of their studies.

So I hit upon an idea: what if we could get a charter bus? A charter bus is comfortable enough to sleep in, large enough to comfortably accommodate our team, and it can drive through the night. If we left on Thursday night and drove back on Sunday night, we would only miss one day of school, while saving two hotel nights. Of course, we had to pay for the bus, but there was great interest on the team: 17 players signed up along with some parents, so we could split that cost many ways.

Upon further reflection, we did not want to arrive in

Nashville too early in the morning. So we decided to leave at midnight. An eight-hour drive would put us in Tennessee's capitol around 8:00 in the morning, just in time for breakfast. Then we could check into our hotel, if the rooms were ready, and relax some before the first round at 1:00.

We had a team meal at a Chinese buffet on Thursday before leaving. All ate a hearty meal and I stood up to give a short speech about the plan. "We have a team room, which will serve as a meeting place for everyone prior to each round. Parents, it will be a place for you to hang out during the rounds, and players, report there after each match so I can review your game and know your result. Let's meet there a half hour before each round for accountability. As you know, we are staying at the Opryland Hotel, one of the largest in the nation that literally covers about a city block. There were over 20 restaurants inside, so there is no excuse for any of you to leave the grounds during the course of the weekend. If you do, you must be accompanied by an adult." That was the discipline portion.

Then I turned to the vision. "This year we have had a fantastic season so far, and everyone in this room is capable of doing something special this weekend. Let's do something special as a team." What that meant exactly, I did not have a firm definition. I continued: "For you seniors, this is your last chance to play on a national stage, so give it all you have."

One of the moms, Pam Norman, chimed in, "Now I wish that I was going!" There were not many questions, so I released the team to finish packing and report to the Bayside parking lot at 11:30 that evening where the bus would be waiting. We loaded up and rumbled off into the night.

Chapter 5

SUPER NATIONALS

Day One

On the bus there were 17 students and four parents. No one was able to go to sleep right away, so I talked individually to the players to make sure each had the proper mindset. I'd ask them questions like, "How are you feeling?" And admonish them to take their time. "You have plenty of time in these games. Make sure you use it." I did not want them to play too fast.

There were also stories coming from the guys who had played at Super Nationals before about some opponents who did not play fair. "What do you mean they didn't play fair?" I asked incredulously.

"Some kids kicked you under the table." replied Jay Smith. "And sometimes they would lie when it was time to report the result and say they won when they really lost."

I have been to six nationals now and have never seen evidence of this behavior, but I still advised my team, "If you run into a dispute, raise your hand and ask for a tournament director. Don't let your opponent talk you into anything."

After some fitful sleep, I awoke around 8:00 near the outskirts of Nashville. We pulled into a Shoney's restaurant for a hot breakfast and made our way to the Opyrland Hotel, just up the road. Despite the early arrival, most of our rooms were ready and we were happy to get another couple of hours of rest on a real bed. I was not interested in the opening ceremonies, instead wanting my players to be focused on their games, and asked the team to report to the team room at noon, one hour before the first round.

When reserving the team room, I requested that a team from another school be assigned with us in order to share the costs. I cannot remember which team it was now, but I do remember that we enjoyed meeting kids from another part of the country, and the parents enjoyed getting to interact with other adults. It is a tradition we have continued at every national we have attended.

Finally, it was time to play and I accompanied the team to the playing hall to help them find their pairings and where they would play. The scene was overwhelming. If you can imagine a warehouse as large as the eye can see with tables and chairs filled with chess boards, that is what it looked like. Again, all age groups were there for a Super Nationals, and at that tournament there were over 5,000 players: the largest rated tournament at that time, ever held in the United States.

Each division was roped off, and coaches were allowed into the playing hall as long as they stayed in the aisles and outside the ropes. This was good if you had a player assigned to a spot around one of the edges, because you could see the board very well. But if you had a player in the middle, if was very difficult to see. Fortunately, I had the foresight to bring my handy dandy binoculars!

We had seven players entered in the U1200 division, six players in the U900, and four in the Unrated. At the high school level, there were two other divisions: U1500 and Open, where the masters play. You could enter as many players as you wanted in a given division, but only the top four cumulative scores count as the team score. Therefore it is to your advantage to enter more than four because if you do and one of your players has a bad tournament, it will not hurt the team score.

The event was paired as an individual tournament, so unlike our other matches where we line up as a team and play side by side, I had players spread all over the playing hall. A nice aspect of this is that players from the same school were ineligible to play each other. Here was the Bayside lineup by pre-tournament rating:

U1200 Team

1161 Sam Davis

1156 Jay Smith

1147 Joey Nickerson

1021 Stephen Smith

944 David Gardner

931 David Mackey

923 J.B. Galle

U900 Team

863 Justin Rabon

834 Chris Nager

685 Matt Shipp

548 Sean Sessel

522 Miles Millar

143 Rico Moorer

Unrated Team

Tim Norman

Colby Parker

John Wnek

Zachary Huey

We were on the national stage, and would be playing kids from across the country from the big chess-playing states. These were not just kids from Alabama and Louisiana. Our opponents ranged from New York to Illinois to Florida to Arizona. How would we perform?

The two rated teams got off to a fast start with perfect 4.0 scores in the first round, while the unrated team got blitzed and lost every game. Technically, this meant that the two rated teams were tied for first place overall, but that thought did not occur to me at this early stage of the event. I am sure there were plenty of other teams right there with us. In the U1200 division there were 60 teams. Of these games, the most critical win, although it would not be known until the end, was J.B. Galle's. While he did not end up as one of the top four scorers for the U1200 team, his win in the first round gave us a 4.0 score that proved to be crucial.

In the second round, the U1200 continued its winning ways by cashing 3.5 out of 4.0 points and ending the day with 7.5 out of 8.0. The U900 team reversed course with everyone losing who won in the first round, with the exception of one draw. This was only good for a half point in the round, leaving us at 4.5 out of 8.0 for the day. The unrated team got on the board with 2.0 points. So as we went to bed that night, the U1200 team was in a tie for first after two rounds, although that idea was still not in my thinking yet. As far as I was concerned, it was a good start and nothing more. While I was pleased that my players were taking their time and that most were doing well in their first national appearance, there were still five long rounds of chess to be played.

Day Two

I have likened the national tournament to running a race in molasses, and the biggest test of stamina is the second day when there are three rounds. That is the potential to play twelve hours of chess if all the games go the distance and my team had done nothing like it before. We came to the team room for breakfast prior to the 9:00 start of round three. I was pleased to note the Bayside parents brought boxes of provisions, and their generosity extended to the players of the team with which we shared the room. As might be expected, there were a couple of teenage boys who dragged in at the last minute for the early morning round, but everyone made it to his assigned seat on time.

In the Swiss system of play, players who win in the first two rounds are matched against players who also have two points in the bag. In other words, the competition gets more difficult as you succeed. And it also works in reverse: if you struggle in the first couple of rounds, you are matched against an opponent with a similar score in the third.

The U900 team, which had a disastrous second round, scored a perfect 4.0 in round three and moved to 8.5 out of 12.0 overall. While they had taken themselves out of any serious consideration for a top tier finish, a top ten or certainly a top twenty was well within reach. The unrated managed another couple of points, and the U1200 continued to grind out victories by posting 3.0 out of 4.0 for a total of 10.5 out of 12.0 Now we were in sole possession of first, paced by the Smith brothers who were each a perfect 3-0.

For the first time I allowed myself to glace at the standings, and I noticed a formidable team nipping at our heels: Porter High School from Brownsville, Texas. They brought a significantly larger team than we did, so they had more potential scorers, and they wore distinctive team shirts that stood out in the sea of players in the main hall. I made a mental note to start observing some of their games.

I also noticed that between rounds, the players from our team roommates kept playing chess among themselves. I wanted my players to get away and take a break from chess between rounds, so I instructed them and those parents who came with them, "Get some physical exercise, get some good food, and get some rest." These were not necessarily in order, and sometimes there was not enough time to do all three. But the larger point was I wanted them to clear their heads and be ready to play for the next round.

Round four was a long one, with some games going the distance. I wish I had a pedometer on me to know how much I walked that day back and forth from the team room to the playing hall and around the aisles of the playing hall trying to see parts of 17 games each round. The unrated team got blitzed again, losing all four games, and I started to joke with them, tongue in cheek, about them walking home to Daphne if they were not able to place for a trophy.

The U900 team managed 1.5 points and I started noticing a pattern with some of these players: they were doing much better with one color than another. For example, a couple of them kept winning with the white pieces and losing with black. It was something I had not noticed during the season when we only played one match per month. But a tournament like this exposes all weaknesses, and I made another note to work on the weaker color with the returning players at future practices.

Meanwhile the U1200 team's sprint had slowed to a jog. We squeezed out two points and now stood at 12.5 out of 16.0 overall, still good for first. Stephen Smith remained unbeaten at 4-0, but Jay got nicked for a draw in a game that went the full four hours. He stopped to have a word with me as he trudged out of the playing hall, a tired look in his eyes. He had less than an hour before the next round, and I told him in the most peppy, upbeat way I could muster, "Get a shower, get some food, and get ready for the next round!"

We were all starting to feel it at that point. While I did not discuss it between rounds with the players, the parents were starting to notice the standings. Calls were made to other parents and administrators back at Bayside with word that the tournament was going well. It was difficult to put a finger on the feeling, but it was kind of like, "Hey, what is going on here?" The sense that something special was happening was palpable. Still, I did not allow myself to dwell on that feeling heading into round five.

The unrated and U900 teams each just managed one point in that round. I gave them encouraging words, told them not to worry about it and to get a good night's sleep. All attention turned to the U1200 team. Unfortunately for Jay, the fourth round game took it out of him and he had no gas left in the tank for the late round five. He lost. Stephen took his first blemish of the event by being held to a draw. David Gardner won and Joey also earned a draw, so we took two points out of four for the round. I later learned that two points in a round usually is not enough to hold your position, but we remained tied for first with Porter with 14.5 points.

It was about 11:00 at night when I raced back to my room to call my wife, who was on maternity leave from Bayside. "How is the baby doing?" I asked.

"Oh she's fine. She is starting to take longer naps and drinking all of her bottle. Mom and Dad are a big help. How is the tournament going?"

"We are in first place after five rounds."

"Really?" She sounded as surprised as I was.

"Can you believe it?" I enthused. "Everything is coming together. It's like the perfect storm, but in a good way." That night I allowed myself to drift to sleep with visions of sugar plums dancing in my head.

Day Three

On Sunday in round six, we came crashing back down to earth. Before I get to that, the U900 and unrated teams had pretty good days. The U900 took four out of eight possible points that day and finished in 14th place overall, a very respectable showing. The unrated team came to play the final day and took seven out of eight possible points. This vaulted them into the top 20, and they proudly took home an 18th place trophy. To me this was quite an accomplishment for a four-player team, and even better, I got what I most wanted: one of the players on this team, sophomore Colby Parker, turned in an impressive performance, going 4-3 and earning a rating of over 1,000. I immediately earmarked him for the varsity team the following year, knowing we were losing eight of the 17 players at Nationals to graduation.

The U1200 team did not fare so well in the early round. Only Joey Nickerson managed a win, with Stephen again drawing, as did David Gardner. This was again only good for two points, which was not enough to hold us in the lead. We had fallen to third with only one round left to play. David's game had gone the distance in time, and he came to me speechless and with the haggard look that was becoming familiar after a marathon game. I knew he liked to drink Red Bull and hoped he could find one before the final round.

Doubt started creeping in. Maybe the mountain was too high for us and we were finally running out of gas. Players were reporting seeing chess pieces in their dreams, so maybe the experience was too much to expect them to actually win it. I walked out of the playing hall, shaking my head and thinking that a National Championship might have just slipped through our fingers.

Back in the team room I saw that I had to get my top coaching game on fast. Panic was starting to set in. I could see the fear in Jay's eyes as he asked me, "Coach, do we still have a chance?"

Summoning all the faux courage I could muster I roared, "Of course we do! Just take care of your game in the final round and we will be fine." I looked each team member in the eye to steady him but inside, I was not sure if it would be enough.

Happily, the final round pairings dealt us a favor. Joey was playing an opponent from the second-place team, and Stephen was matched against a player from the first-place team, Porter.

This allowed us a chance to make up ground and at least control a piece of our own destiny. Had we not had these direct match ups, we would have needed more help from the opponents of the teams ahead of us.

I collected myself and headed back to the playing hall. I figured we would be in for a long four hours and as I strolled around glancing at games, I was presented with a very pleasant surprise: Joey was *demolishing* his opponent! I'm not sure his game even lasted one hour, and what a boost. That win by itself was probably enough to push us into second place. Joey finished with five of a possible seven points for the tournament and took home an individual trophy as he tied for 25th place out of more than 300 kids in the division.

Tournament chess is nothing if not a roller coaster ride of emotions. Not long after, I learned that David Gardner lost, no doubt a mental victim of his epic round six clash. Coming into round seven, only four of our players were in position to score for the team, so that one hurt. It all came down to the Smith brothers.

Jay was Mr. Endgame, so it was no surprise his game was going down to the wire. No doubt his experience served him well and he pulled out the win. Not long after, Stephen cashed in with a narrow, critical win over his Porter opponent. This gave him an undefeated tournament with five wins and two draws for a total of six points of seven for the event: good enough for seventh place individually in the division. We had three points in the final round. Would it be enough?

The agonizing part was the wait. I stayed in the playing hall trying to determine how the other Porter kids had done. I knew that their top four scorers going into the round had only managed about two points, but it was entirely possible they had other players who won in the final round and put themselves into the top four scorers for the team. Even every half point was precious and crucial.

The game tabulators who assisted the tournament directors sat around the side of the playing hall, and I went to the ones who were responsible for the U1200 division. "Any results from the Porter players?' I asked eagerly. The were able to show me a few, some wins, some losses, but without knowing the cumulative score for each player, it did not mean much.

So I walked up to the Porter coach and asked him: "Hey Coach, any players for you scoring in the final round that might put them in the top four?" He was holding a piece of paper with all his players and their results on it, which was quite full by then. He scratched his head and did not seem to think so. It appeared that we had done it. Zachary Huey's dad, Mike, claims to have seen me skip out of the playing hall.

We still did not know for sure, so a few of us camped out in the lobby outside one of the playing halls. It was there that the tournament organizers brought out large cork boards on tripod stands between rounds with the current standings and the pairings for the next round. Since the tournament was over, they were only bringing out the final standings prior to the awards ceremony. Finally, about an hour after the final round ended, the parade of boards began.

A surge of interested people pressed toward the boards as they were being set in place, and I shamelessly jumped in front of the group, employing my best rebound block out technique from basketball playing days. I settled in front of the U1200 board and scanned the team standings. It read: 1. Bayside Academy. We were National Champions! I whooped and hollered and high fived with my team.

In fairness, it was a co-National Championship. Both Bayside and Porter finished tied with 19.5 points. In this case, computer tiebreakers go into effect to determine the winner. For national events, four different tiebreaks are employed in a pre-determined order of preference, and Bayside won all four of them.

To give you an example of a couple of them, the first is called the Cumulative tiebreaker. This gives more weighting to those who win early round games on the theory that because of those wins, they faced tougher competition in later rounds. And recall, we got off to a very fast start as a team in the early rounds. The second is called the Solkoff tiebreaker, which measures strength of opposition by adding all the points scored by each opponent. A final example is called Kashdan, which awards four points for each win, two for a draw, and one for a loss and showed we had more wins along the way than Porter.

Any way you sliced it, in other words, Bayside came out on top. I was so proud of the team and especially for three notable accomplishments:

We became the first chess team in history to win a National Championship from Alabama.

Collectively for the 17 players that came, we had a plus score, meaning that we won more games than we lost. Our total record for the event was 53, wins, 50 losses, and 16 draws.

We netted a boat load of rating points. Not including the unrated team, our players collectively came out of the tournament with over 1,050 rating points that we took from other players from other states at our first Nationals.

The awards ceremony seemed to take forever to start and last even longer once it began, mainly because there were so many awards to give: individual and team. Then when our time finally came, it only lasted a moment. What a feeling it was to stand on stage with my team and accept the first-place trophy. I was a new dad and a National Champion. It does not get much better.

On the Bus and Reception Home

The bus was idling for us outside the hotel and it was time to take another journey through the night. The plan was to hit Bayside around 6:00 the next morning. Whether the players actually went to class was between them and their parents, but at least I was going to make sure they were there in time. At any rate, I figured they would sleep well that night!

Before we turned off the lights, it was time for another brief speech from me, the first part of which I loosely modeled on the one quarterback Steve Young gave after the San Francisco 49ers won the Super Bowl following the 1994 season. "Hey, Bayside!" it began. "You just won a National Championship!"

Cheers and applause broke out from the back of the bus.

"This is an accomplishment that no one can ever take away from you for the rest of your lives!"

More cheering and applause.

Then, because I did not want them to get too carried away and because our season was not yet over, I shouted, rather harshly, "Practice on Thursday!"

Moans and groans came from the back. Whenever I get together with members of this team, even today, we still laugh about that speech.

Word had preceded us and when we pulled into the Bayside parking lot the next morning, we were met by parents and girlfriends of the team. It was a bigger reception than I imagined, and I knew we had to publicize our accomplishment while it was still fresh. At the moment, I decided to devote thought to that later because I wanted to get a couple more hours of rest before going into work.

The PR Circuit

Previously when we had won as State Champions, we made an appearance before the Daphne City Council and received a proclamation from the Mayor. This clearly called for more. We still appeared before the city, but we took it a few steps farther.

First in line was an appearance before the Baldwin County Commission. We took the kids out of school for about half the morning one day and drove up to the county seat of Bay Minette, about a 40-minute drive. Appearing before the commission carries the added bonus of being seen on the local cable access television channel, and appearing before them was a nice recognition for the team.

Bayside then threw a pep rally for us and invited our state senator, Bradley Byrne, to appear and say a few words. Senator Byrne brought a resolution from the Alabama State Senate in honor of the chess team's achievement. "We are used to winning college football National Championships in Alabama." said Senator Byrne. "There is no reason for not winning them in other areas as well."

The rally was in the Student Activity Center (SAC), where we play our home matches, and on the wall hung State Championship banners from 2002 and 2004. That day we unveiled a National Championship banner that now hangs beside them. It was beyond gratifying to stand in front of the student body and hear the cheers of approval for their chess team.

News coverage came as well. The local paper, the *Mobile Press-Register,* ran an editorial stating that all too often they felt called to point out shortcomings in the educational system, but that Bayside's championship was a hopeful sign. Local television news cameras came to campus and did a story, too. After the news visit, Bayside assembled the chess team, took a photo, and had it framed and engraved as a gift to the players and coach. I treasure this momento.

After the 2002 State Championship, we ordered rings for the team, paid for by the players, but with a discount through the school. We did not order any in 2004 because most of the players were the same. The engraved photo served that purpose in 2005.

Deciding to strike while the iron was hot, I made an appointment with Tom Johnson, the headmaster. I requested that the position of chess coach be compensated equivalent to the stipend that a coach for any other sport is paid at the school. I insisted that the position has value, regardless of who holds it. Mr. Johnson agreed, and my days as a volunteer coach were over. I was now a professional!

I made efforts for regional and national coverage to no avail. For example, I called Paul Finebaum who had a syndicated sports radio show running throughout the Southeast. He had actually been to some chess events and remarked on the intensity of the competition, but he declined my pitch.

I even wrote e-mails to some national talk shows like Conan O'Brien and David Letterman. In Conan's case, he had done a funny skit about an Alabama bumpkin playing checkers on his back porch against his dog. My pitch to him was that in fairness, how about having some successful chess-playing students from Alabama on the show? I never heard a response.

No matter. We knew what we had accomplished. To go from no program to a National Championship in five years to me seemed nothing less than remarkable. I thought I had reached the pinnacle of what could be accomplished as a chess coach.

Again, I was wrong.

Bayside Academy parents hanging out in the Team Room during one of the rounds. We found having a team room to be indispensable as a gathering place before rounds to ensure accountability and that each player had something to eat. Those parents and players without a team room were left to hang out in the hallways between rounds as the individual rooms were very far away from the playing halls.

The High School playing hall at Super Nationals III, Gaylord Opryland Hotel, Nashville, Tennessee. There were two other playing halls of similar size for the junior high and elementary sections. Over 5,000 players participated in the event - at the time the largest rated tournament in U.S. history

The National Champs receiving their trophy. From l-r: Stephen Smith, Sam Davis, Joey Nickerson, Jay Smith, J.B. Galle, David Mackey, Coach Eric Nager, a U.S. Chess Federation official. Stephen and Joey are holding individual trophies they won for their performance in the tournament.

Bayside Players who went to Super Nationals III in 2005. Front row l-r: Sean Sessel, Miles Millar, David Gardner*, Matt Shipp; 2nd row l-r: Colby Parker, Zachary Huey, John Wnek, Joey Nickerson*, Tim Norman, Chris Nager, David Mackey*; Back row l-r: Hector Takahashi, Justin Rabon, Stephen Smith*, Sam Davis*, Rico Moorer, J.B. Galle*, Jay Smith*, Coach Eric Nager. (*denotes member of National Championship U1200 team) The school presented this photo to the team with the engraving, "Bayside Academy 2005 State & National Chess Champions"

Chapter 6

RUSSIA

We entered the 2005-2006 season with some uncertainty. We had three returning players from the National Championship team: David Gardner, Stephen Smith, and Joey Nickerson. While Colby Parker had proved himself at Nationals as ready to step up to the varsity team on fourth board, I had no idea who was going to play first board. So we had an open competition in practice leading up to the first match.

Sentimentally, I leaned toward David because he was a senior and had been with the program from the beginning. Based on the previous year's performance, Stephen looked like the strongest player, going undefeated at Nationals. But Joey separated himself from the others and clearly earned the position. He had gone to summer chess camp and played in rated tournaments, and the improvement was noticeable. Not to take anything away from Joey, but some of the spark for chess seemed to have drained out of Stephen.

We needed all of them playing at their best because we were tested immediately: the season opener came against ASMS. I do not like playing our fiercest rival before anyone else, and to make matters worse, their team featured sophomore Landon

Sykora who had starred for us. It was so difficult to coach against one of our former smartest and best players, compounded by the fact that we greatly missed his family as supporters of the program.

One year we had our season ending team party at Landon's house. Another year for the state tournament, Landon's dad, Glen, drove his church bus for us. And Landon's mom, Tampa, was a pillar for our program, once remarking about me to others, "He coaches chess like he gets paid $100,000 to do it."

I dropped Stephen to third board where he played Landon and lost. The rest of the team hung on to win by the narrowest possible margin in a 4-player match: 2-1-1. From there, we were able to coast the rest of the way to our third consecutive league title by beating every other opponent 4-0. It was not quite the perfect 24-0-0 record from the previous year, but 22-1-1 is not too bad, either. Joey won the Morphy. We also won our fourth consecutive county title.

Chess for Peace

As the season was going and we were looking ahead to state, I read an invitation to all scholastic players in the U.S. to join a team headed to Russia in March to participate in a program called Chess for Peace. This was the brainchild of former World Champion Anatoly Karpov, who I was told at the time traveled 300 days per year around the world to promote chess as a way for people and nations to get along better with one another.

As an aside on Karpov, many Americans remember the great U.S. World Champion Bobby Fischer, who held the crown from 1972-1975. This was the height of the Cold War, and

Russian players had dominated the top ranks of professional chess for decades. To have an American beat them at their own game was a tremendous accomplishment. However, Bobby was a little eccentric to say the least, and he declined to defend the title. It then fell to Karpov who held it for about a decade.

The idea of traveling to Russia intrigued me, so I got in touch with Mikhail Korenman, the domestic coordinator, who at the time lived in Lindsborg, Kansas. He said the trip would be one week long, and cost about $1,500 per player, including round trip airfare from New York, hotel accommodations, and two meals per day. This sounded like an incredible deal, so I brought it up to the team and we had ten enthusiastic takers: Joey and his dad, Stephen and his dad, David, Colby and both of his parents, and Zachary Huey and his mom.

We later learned that only 26 U.S. players were going, so Bayside's five made up a significant portion of Team USA. Mikhail coordinated all of our visas, and we were responsible for our own domestic airfare to and from New York. The trip was beyond anything I imagined as a coach, and never anticipated that some of my duties would include those of an international travel agent!

First, I had to coordinate my own travel. The weekend the team left, I was attending a niece's wedding in Florida, so I hopped on a plane the next day and joined the team one day late. They were eating lunch as I arrived, and I noticed the hotel was somewhat less than five-star. In fact, a couple of the parents relocated to a nicer place. But I did not mind because I was there for the experience.

We had our first match that afternoon, and the U.S. players were still recovering from jet lag. It showed in their games as the Russians defeated us. I noticed that in order to make the games more evenly matched, the Russians gave us opponents who were younger than our players. Chess is very serious there and is taught as a math subject nationally in the schools. No wonder their test scores are higher than ours!

While most of them did not speak English, we shared the common language of chess. Also, all U.S. players brought small, distinctive gifts from home that they swapped with their Russian counterparts before each game. Some examples were jars of peanut butter, flags, or small cowboy hats.

The Russian fare at the hotel consisted mostly of beet dishes, which many of our players did not like. Fortunately, there was a Pizza Hut near the hotel for late night carb loading. Still, there were other areas of Russian culture everyone did enjoy. For example, Russians are known for their acrobats, and one night we took in a performance of the Moscow circus. Another day we toured the Kremlin and Red Square.

In some respects, the game of chess was the least portion of the trip, given that we only played four matches over seven days. One day we loaded up on a bus and drove outside the city to the seat of the Eastern Orthodox Church: their equivalent of the Vatican. There we saw worshipers come and pray, and the monks prepared an organic meal for us.

Even though the trip was in March, it was a fantastic opportunity to do some Christmas shopping. Vendors were plentiful on the Moscow streets, and we found classic Russian gifts, like nesting dolls. Some of the parents brought back some vodka.

Finally, we buckled down to play some more chess, and as a team lost the second match to the Russians. For that event we played at a club named after Tigran Petrosian, the former World Champion. Before the match began, the players were told to adjust their clocks to a shorter time control. We had to be out of the building by a certain time because an adult league was coming in to play after us. In Russia they play chess like we bowl in the United States!

Sometimes before a match, we would get treated to a chess lecture by a Russian master. I say "treated" because it was a treat for me. I am not sure how the players felt about it. One thing I have learned in life though, is that there is very little better than hearing a lecture on chess spoken with a Russian accent: "If 'dis happens, it's draw."

Traveling with a Master

For the trip, Mikhail had lined up our own star power to accompany Team USA: Susan Polgar, at one time the greatest female chess player in the world. At the time she was living in New York. She flew with us, stayed in our hotel, and went with us to all the matches and tourist attractions. After the matches, she helped analyze the players' games.

One of her major initiatives is to get more girls playing chess at a young age. To that end, she has organized many tournaments featuring separate sections just for girls. Her theory is that girls might be less intimidated to play if they get to play each other when they are just starting out, and that approach seems to be successful. Susan hosts an annual camp and tournament in St. Louis with the female State Champions from around the country. There are also automatic qualifiers from regional tournaments she hosts. My daughter, Nicole, attended one of these for three years running in New Orleans and won her section one year, qualifying for Susan's event.

From our trip, Susan went on to be the chess coach at Texas Tech University where she founded the Susan Polgar Institute for Chess Excellence (SPICE). She won some collegiate National Championships there before moving on to Webster University in St. Louis where she resides today. Her sisters are renowned chess players as well.

Socializing with Susan is absolutely delightful. She is warm and personable, but when it comes time to play chess, she is all business. One day near the end of our trip she put on a simultaneous exhibition against all 26 scholastic players on our team. She dresses immaculately, and her expression is stoic as she goes from board to board to make her move. Her record at the end was a perfect 26 wins, no losses, and no draws.

Another master who made the trip was Life Master Robert Haines from New Mexico, my roommate at the hotel. A Life Master is someone who has attained the rating of Master (2200) and held it for at least 300 rated games. One of Robert's pupils went on the trip with his dad and Robert accompanied them. He gave me many great stories and inspiration for how to be a better chess coach. I was so impressed that I invited him to Alabama the following year to work with my team. We formed other fast friendships with some of the other members of our team. Coach Billy Willson of Regis Jesuit near Denver, brought five or six players and I still keep in touch with him as well.

Of course, the biggest name of all who we met was former World Champion Anatoly Karpov. He came to address our team and we had opportunity to take photos with him. We even saw the table at which he played his World Championship match against Gary Kasparov in the 1980s with the flags and the name plates still in place.

Maybe all that chess started rubbing off on us, because the American players won their final two matches against the Russians. And I am happy to report that each of the five Bayside players won at least one game of the four during the trip. I even got in on the action as, during the final match, there were more Russians than Americans, so I slid into a board so that the Russian student would have someone to play. Perhaps he was nervous playing an adult, or he wanted to be polite to a guest, but in either case, I won the game.

The weather while we were in Moscow was dull, cold, and gray, but the hospitality we experienced from our hosts, the friendships we made, and the stories we brought home to tell brightened everyone who participated. As we flew home, I realized again how I had underestimated what could be accomplished as a scholastic chess coach in Alabama. Not only had we won State Championships and a National Championship, but we had represented our country in international competition. That is a privilege I will never forget.

P.S.

A postscript to the trip was that we still had a state tournament to play in Tuscaloosa, Alabama. With all the great experience we had in Russia, I thought there was no way we could be stopped from winning our third consecutive title. But things do not always go as planned.

The day of the state team championship conflicted with the Bayside prom, and my players wanted to attend this social function. Tuscaloosa is about a four-hour drive from Daphne one way, so there was no way to make it back in time by car. So I called Rodney Pilot, a member of Bayside's board. He had once told me that if I ever needed anything, I should ask him. It was then time to put that offer to the test. Rodney had a private airplane he kept at the Mobile airport. "Rodney, do you remember when you said to ask if I needed anything?" I started the conversation hesitantly.

"Yes." he replied calmly.

"Well, the state tournament is in Tuscaloosa on Saturday and I want to get the kids back in time for prom. May we use your plane?"

"I'll have it gassed up and ready to go for you that morning. The pilot will meet you there."

But that was not the end of the obstacles to success. Unknown to any of us, Stephen had played his last game for Bayside on the Russia trip. He declined to make the trip to state and did not come back for his senior year. This was devastating to lose such an experienced player, even if he was not having his best year. I had every confidence in plugging Zachary Huey, who also went to Russia, into fourth board, but we were not going with our best possible team.

Another obstacle was sophomore Jeremy Cooper, the first board at Foley High. He had burst onto the scene in league play and is the kind of player you love to coach but hate coaching against. This is because he makes all the players on his team better and I was trying desperately to recruit him to Bayside. It would have been a natural fit because his dad worked in Daphne and they could have driven together each day. However, he wanted to stay with his friends. Joey defeated him in the regular season, but it was not an easy win.

All of these factors conspired to make the tournament a painful and excruciating experience. We lost the first two rounds to Foley and John Carroll by the narrowest of margins, and by somewhat controversial tournament director calls that went against us. Gerald Larson was the new Vice President of Scholastics within the Alabama Chess Federation, and as such directed the state tournaments. He was tough but fair, and a tremendous improvement over the previous directors with whom we dealt. That did not make his decisions any easier to swallow.

One of them involved the position on the board at the conclusion of Joey and Jeremy's game. It looked to me that it should have been a draw, which would have drawn the match, but the director ruled that Joey had run out of time on his clock a split second before that position on the board was achieved. The other decision involved David Gardner against his John Carroll opponent, and it did not help our cause that David mouthed off to the director. We had rarely lost two matches in a season, let alone in one day. The only bright spot for him was that he won his final round game, which was the last of his Bayside career as the pilots were pressuring us to get out of there ahead of the coming storm.

I was left in the uncomfortable position of having to congratulate the John Carroll coach for winning the tournament. I did so sincerely, because it is the right thing to do. But I felt a tremendous sense of responsibility for letting a team from northern Alabama take the title on our watch.

The good news was that the plane made it back in time. As we touched down on the Fairhope airport runway, we could see the boys' mothers standing by with tuxedos in hand to take their sons to get cleaned up and dressed for the prom. While the state tournament result left a very sour taste in our mouth that lasted all summer, we had nonetheless taken our program to another incredible level with the Russia trip.

We had to be content with that.

St. Basil's Cathedral, Red Square, Moscow. On the right is Lenin's Mausoleum. As a member of the U.S. Army Reserve who joined the military during the tail end of the Cold War, it was a particular thrill for me to witness the Westernization of Russian society symbolized by the European sports cars zipping around the city and the stocked shelves in the stores.

Making new friends. Mikhail Korenman (left) organized the Chess for Peace trip. There I met Billy Willson (center), the chess coach at Regis Jesuit near Denver, Colorado, and two of his players as part of Team USA.

Jet-lagged U.S. players. Bayside players Colby Parker (left) and Zachary Huey (center) struggle to stay awake in first round action against their Russian opponents. There is an 8-hour time difference between Moscow and Daphne, Alabama. Team USA lost the first match but rallied for an overall 2-2 score against the Russians.

Analyzing a game. Grandmaster Susan Polgar analyzes Bayside player Zachary Huey's game as I look on. We take notation of all of our games so they can be reviewed for lessons learned.

86

World Champion match. The table where Gary Kasparov battled Anatoly Karpov for the world chess championship. Each men held the title at one time and are symbolic of the seriousness with which Russians play chess.

Chess Royalty. Mikhail Korenman introduces Team USA to former World Champion Anatoly Karpov, accompanied by Grandmaster Susan Polgar. Mr. Karpov established the Chess for Peace initiative and at the time was traveling 300 days per year around the world promoting chess.

Bayside Academy with the Champ. The Bayside players who went to Russia with former World Champion. From l-r: David Gardner, Stephen Smith, Colby Parker, Joey Nickerson, Anatoly Karpov, Eric Nager.

Moscow street vendors show their wares with traditional Russian nesting dolls. Although our trip was in March, many of us completed our Christmas shopping early that year.

The Russian Orthodox Church. A major portion of our trip was taking in the sights. We took a day trip to this church where a meal of organically grown foods was prepared for us by monks. Other sights included the circus and the ballet.

Simultaneous Exhibition. Grandmaster Susan Polgar took on all 26 members of Team USA in a simultaneous exhibition. Her score against them? A perfect 26-0-0. Here she victimizes Bayside player David Gardner.

Chapter 7

A STEP BACK

David Gardner was an irreplaceable loss. He was the only player to be with the program for each of the first six years of existence, and he left with 67 career wins: most all time and a record that still stands today as of this writing. Joey Nickerson and Colby Parker returned in 2006-2007 for their senior year on the varsity team, but I still had two openings.

One was filled by freshman Kevin Nelson, a fresh Christ the King graduate who I had had my eye on for some time. He also brought his younger brother, Blake, with him early from Christ the King as a seventh grader. Sixth grader Wesley Dean came out for the team, and he and Blake frequently interrupted our practices by annoying each other, but their relationship is a story for later in the book. I still needed a fourth board.

There were still a few players remaining from the Nashville trip two years before, and senior Rico Moorer was one of them. He had played on the U900 team and he earned the fourth spot on the roster. League play began that year with a win over Foley, as we paid them back for the loss at state in the spring. We went on to our fourth straight league title and Joey defended the Morphy, but not without difficulty.

We hosted the last match of the season that year and were paired against UMS. We had already clinched the title as a team, but the Morphy was still in the balance. That year UMS had a standard for their players such that if you won at least four games on the varsity team, you earned a coveted varsity letter. Joey's opponent that round had three wins so far that year, and was not intimidated by Joey's status as the best player in the league. In fact, he pushed Joey around the board for much of the game and had a winning position before Joey started to take him seriously and drew on his vast experience in big games to pull out some tactics and prevail. While he occasionally took an opponent lightly, there were few better game closers at Bayside than Joey.

Unhappily, Daphne surprised us in the county tournament, and we failed to defend our title there. Then it was onto state, that year in Greenville. I never like to rely too heavily on seniors, preferring to develop younger talent for our future, and that year we had three seniors on varsity. The following year was starting to look scary, so I stepped up recruiting efforts. My top target was Michael Tran, one of the top players for Fairhope, and his mother was the school nurse at Bayside. Sadly, Bayside seemed unwilling to work out a creative solution and he never came on board.

Looking ahead as I did caused me to make a decision that in hindsight I deeply regret: leaving Rico off the varsity roster for state. I took a younger player instead, and that was no way to treat him or his friends on the team who did not care for my call. Rico, I apologize.

As it was, we struggled to tie Foley and ASMS. Jeremy defeated Joey and finally surpassed him as the top player in our region. In the last round Foley played ASMS and we needed them to tie each other in order to end up in a three-way tie as State Champions. I recall the helpless feeling of watching players I did not coach battle it out and needing help from them in order to secure our spot. The superior play of Jeremy's team prevailed, and they beat ASMS 3-1. Foley was the new State Champion. Bayside settled for second. While that was not the way I wanted the rest of our seniors to end their careers, the storm clouds over our program were just beginning to gather.

A Faculty Sponsor

Something must have happened at Bayside during the 2006-2007 academic year, because the summer afterward it was announced that all extra-curricular programs must have a faculty sponsor. Until this point I had been a one-man show as coach, so the news delighted me. Finally the chess team would have a full time advocate on campus who would raise the profile of our program and keep us from having to fight for resources. The sponsor could also help with recruiting and building the program. Or so I thought.

My initial optimism was buoyed by what Tom Johnson, the headmaster, told me. He said the new sponsor, who was moving to the area from another state, had experience working with chess programs. I was elated and could not wait to meet her. When I did, it was a crushing disappointment. She had no experience working with chess and did not seem to have much interest doing so. Our initial conversation at the first practice went something like this: "Welcome to Bayside." I said. "I'm looking forward to working with you and we have enjoyed a lot of success as a program."

"How often do you practice?" she asked.

"Every Thursday to block out the time because our matches are on Thursdays."

"How long do you practice?"

"Two hours: from 3:30-5:30."

"Let's shorten that to 90 minutes. I need to go by 5:00."

"But it's only once a week." I protested. "We need the work."

"We end at 5:00." she decided arbitrarily. "Oh, and no kids younger than 4th grade."

"Why not?" At this point I was incredulous.

"I don't want to deal with younger kids."

"But we already have a returning player who is younger than that." I prevailed in that portion of the argument, and he was allowed to continue with the team, but no other young players were allowed.

A pall descended over the program. I am sure the kids could sense the tension between me and the sponsor, and that did not help us in recruiting new players and performing at our best. In fairness to the sponsor, she was probably told something like the chess program needed to be reigned in, so she was acting in obedience to that. Still, if the roles were reversed and I was coming into sponsoring a very successful program, there is no question I would be very deferential to the coach, especially if I was not familiar with the game.

Part of her attitude might have stemmed from directives she probably was given about any type of club activities taking place off campus. This was no longer supposed to happen. However, I disclosed up front that often on Saturday mornings, I would go to a local bookstore or coffee shop to have a beverage. While there, a player or two might join me and go over some chess games. For that to continue I needed to get written permission from the parents, which I readily did.

An uneasy truce ensued as we embarked upon the worst season in Bayside chess history. The varsity went 4-2 in the regular season with losses to ASMS and Christ the King. With the latter loss, I knew we did not have the horses to go to state that year. For the first and only time ever, we did not place in our own league.

To compensate for my frustration, I threw myself into other activities. That fall I started a course that coincided with the school year called Leadership Baldwin County. It was for professionals from different walks of life and different locations in the county who were already leaders in their communities to come together and address common problems. I thoroughly enjoyed it and made several new friends.

Next, I applied to be appointed to fill a position on our city council when the incumbent resigned with about a year left in her term. About seven other candidates also applied and we were each interviewed by the other members of the council. In the end they selected me and I served the rest of the term.

Checklist for Checkmate

One of the most therapeutic activities for me is writing. So another project I threw myself into was writing a book about our experience winning a National Title in chess. I thought our story deserved to be told, and it that it should be something Hollywood would love! So I shopped the concept around to a couple of domestic publishers. After getting rejection notices, I considered self-publishing.

Before I went that route, I spoke to a Life Master who lived in a nearby town, and he told me about a publisher in London that was friendly to chess. I soon contacted Grand Master Ray Keene of Impala Press by email and told him of my proposed project. He was interested and agreed to take it on so I started writing.

In an attempt to appeal to a broader audience than just chess enthusiasts, I wrote the book as a business title, the full name of which is *Checklist for Checkmate: 15 Keys to Building a Successful Team.* I identified 15 lessons that we learned along the way about leadership and team building, and made each one a chapter. Then I would focus like a laser on each chapter and bat out to what amounted to a five to ten-page paper on each, sometimes in one sitting.

People have asked me how long it takes to write a book. In that case with concerted effort, I knocked out the first draft over Christmas break within a couple of weeks. From a chess standpoint, I only told the story of winning the National

Championship in the introduction and illustrated leadership points with various examples and anecdotes drawn from the team. But it was not a comprehensive history of the program as this book is.

Ray insisted that the book contain the notation from some actual games my team played, and because I keep a copy of most of them, it was easy to cull through and select the most meaningful ones that also happened to be complete and legible. The last portion of that criteria eliminated some games I would like to have used!

Ray's team proofread the manuscript, laid it out and did the cover design. By the spring it rolled off the presses. Impala had it placed on Amazon and Ray wrote a nice review. While it was a thrill to have my first book published, it was expensive because of the distance and exchange rate to get my book printed and shipped to this country.

A few years later I updated the book with an addendum, and at that point asked Ray if I could look into getting it printed domestically. I had retained all rights to it and he readily agreed. I soon found the friendly folks at Southeastern Press in nearby Mobile to do the work in a much more convenient and cost-effective way. Still, I will always be grateful to Ray Keene for giving me a chance. Thanks, Ray!

I have since given many talks on the book to civic groups, college alumni groups, and even one to the Bayside Academy board after enough turnover had taken place that I was concerned nobody knew our story. Each time I emphasize the story about how we built our program from scratch to winning a National Title, figuring that anyone who wants to learn the lessons we did can read the book. Finally, a member of the audience told me one time that the story should be its own book, so here it is!

Administration Support

Meanwhile back in our difficult chess season, things came to a head. One Saturday, I was working with a couple of players, as usual, and a few more happened to walk into the same bookstore and wanted to play. I certainly was not going to turn them away, and it only happened that one time. Somehow word got back to the sponsor, and she took it to mean that I was having large practices every week. She did not believe me when I told her what actually happened.

The situation was starting to be more than I wanted to handle, and I seriously considered resigning as coach. Credit for being a rock of support and talking me out of it was our Team Mom, Jennifer Nelson, Kevin and Blake's mother. She knew I was going through a rough time and she gave me words of encouragement every time she saw me. "Hang in there Coach, we need you!" she frequently said.

"Jennifer, this year is not very much fun." I'd responded soberly.

"But don't you enjoy being with the kids? Why would you not want to stay?" she asked.

"I do enjoy that, but we have set a standard of excellence here, and we need to maintain that. I do not want to be associated with a program that is not allowed to be excellent." By that I meant excellence in quality, not necessarily in results.

"I understand that." she said with a knowing pause. "But things can turn around." Thanks to her I stayed, and I am glad I did.

The last straw came at the end of the season. The regular season ended with Foley in first place and the rest of the league consoling itself that Jeremy Cooper was a senior and none of us would have to face him again. Bayside was not going to state, but the county tournament was coming up, and it would be great practice for our younger kids. Prior to our last practice before county, the sponsor started in, "We are not going to county."

"Why not?" I asked, wearily this time. "It's right here in town, so we don't even have to travel."

"Our season ends Thursday."

That was it. It was time to go to Mr. Johnson, but she beat me to the punch by resigning as faculty sponsor. At work I received an ominous call that Mr. Johnson wanted to meet with me. What had she told him?

I drove to Bayside and as I pulled into the parking lot, I recall thinking that it was possible I could be let go as coach. I did not step out of the car until I came to mental peace about the situation. I knew that I had done nothing wrong.

My first stop was the library to see the sponsor. She did not want to talk and told me Mr. Johnson was waiting for me in his office. As I stepped in to see him, I was immediately put at ease by his laid-back manner. "The faculty sponsor has resigned." he told me.

"Yes, I know. I just heard." I responded.

"So what was the deal with Saturday practice?" he asked matter of factly.

"Well, I worked with just a couple of kids at a time, with written permission from the parents as you requested. One time a few extra players showed up and I let them stay."

There was a prolonged silence that I'm sure seemed longer than it was. "What is left of the season?" he finally asked.

"We have the county tournament coming up and I'd like to take a team."

He then looked me square in the eye. "I will be your faculty sponsor for that. We will find a new sponsor for you next year." I walked out of his office on air. The headmaster backed me up at a most critical time. All the hard work and long hours were recognized and appreciated.

I went back to the library, not knowing what to expect. I told the sponsor that Mr. Johnson was going to serve in that capacity, and she did not visibly react. I then told her I had no hard feelings and I sincerely wished her well.

Looking back, the whole thing was unfortunate and avoidable because it seems we were each misinformed from the beginning about the other, so our relationship never started off on the right foot. I do forgive her and do not hold a grudge because she was doing the best she knew how under difficult circumstances. In a different setting, I like to think we could be friends.

We only took a middle school team to county and did not win anything. Other than blowing my stack at Blake for resigning a game when he had no business doing so, it was an enjoyable day, free of the stress of the rest of that season. I liked that Mr. Johnson was there to see us in action firsthand and observe how the students and I interact.

Looking ahead to the next year though, it seemed like our program was in shambles. Just three years removed from a National Championship, we had failed to place in our league and did not field a varsity team at county. The fall had been sharp and sudden.

I was about to learn that building back again can happen just as fast.

P.S. *About that Faculty Sponsor*

Not all stories have a happy ending, but this one does. That sponsor remained at Bayside, and while our paths did not have reason to cross over the years, whenever I saw her from a distance there was a sense of awkwardness. Years later, my daughter was in her class. She approached me at the meet the teacher event and said she did not want there to be anything between us, and finally explained to me the guidance she was given, not from the head of school, but from the head of the upper division.

I told her it was all forgiven and forgotten as far as I was concerned. I thanked her for sharing that with me and my hope is that we can go forward as friends. It was all a big, impersonal misunderstanding and the overall lesson for me is that it's important to keep your heart and mind open to others with whom you have had a less than pleasant experience. You don't always know what they had to go through.

Chapter 8

BUILDING BACK AGAIN

The Perfect Faculty Sponsor

What a difference the right faculty sponsor makes! As the 2008-2009 season opened, Mr. Johnson assigned 4th grade teacher Sally Kalaris as the Chess Team Sponsor. Sally's daughter, Sarah, had played for the team a few years earlier so Sally had an appreciation for the program. Also, as a teacher of younger kids, she was in position to recruit from the elementary school, as well as discipline when necessary – something I struggled with sometimes with the younger players.

It was a perfect match. Sally at once got busy placing chess events on the school calendar and advocating for our share of funds raised through the annual golf tournament and other avenues. Eventually she helped write and track contracts for the students and parents to sign, outlining expectations for being a member of the team. Her moral support and enthusiasm have been blessings beyond measure, and they all came with the added bonus of support from her husband, George. I refer to him as the First Man of Bayside Chess.

With the right attitude guiding the program, players flocked back to it. Among the fresh talent that year were the Dahlkes, Scott and Greg, who had relocated with their family from Louisiana; the Runels brothers, Trey and Will; junior Hayden Gunn, and sophomore Matt Cazalas. And the returning players, like 8th grader Eric Peterson, had worked hard on their games over the summer. Eric was a dramatic case of a player who went from someone I thought barely knew how to coordinate an attack as a 7th grader to earning first board on the junior high team.

Thus, reloaded we promptly returned to the top of the league, but not in the way I expected. The varsity team, anchored by Matt, Kevin, and Trey, fought to an undefeated record but had two ties. This was only good for second place in a format where all teams competed together. In other words, A teams were mixed with B and C teams. Meanwhile, the junior high team of Eric, Wesley Dean, Will, and Scott quietly dismantled everyone they played en route to a perfect 6-0 record with only one board loss, for a total overall of 23-1-0. This earned them the league championship and we finished 1-2 as we did in the 2004 season, only this time it was with the younger team on top. Eric Peterson won the Morphy to boot.

The rapid turnaround was dizzying in speed and continued into the county tournament where we tied for first with Fairhope. While we did not know it at the time, that was the last Baldwin County Tournament because of changes that came to our league the following year. In nine years of competition, Bayside finished first or tied for first five times.

The state tournament did not turn out so well. In 2006 we lost two matches in one day at state, which was the worst day to date of Bayside chess. The 2009 tournament topped that as we lost all three matches we played that day to Indian Springs, John Carroll, and Bob Jones of Huntsville, the eventual champion. While we had skipped state the year before, new coaches had moved into northern Alabama and raised the playing level for that part of the state. The southern champion of our league was no longer an automatic winner. We clearly had more work to do.

There were still two bright spots from the weekend, however. The first is that Bayside finally had its first individual state champion: 4th grader Trent Kannegieter. Trent had tied for first in his division and lost the first place trophy on tiebreaks, but as is the case in chess where a tie at the top is not an uncommon occurrence, Trent still shared the *title* of State Champion. It was a very proud moment.

And we did not return empty handed in terms of hardware. I had registered an elementary team for the team tournament, but we ended up being the only team in the section when the tournament began. As such, we were *awarded* the Elementary School State Championship, even though we did not win it over the board. What is the old saying about a large percentage of success in life is in just showing up? While that was not the way we prefer to win them, it was our sixth overall State Championship trophy as a program and the first since 2005. It was time to go back to Nashville for Super Nationals.

Super Nationals IV, Nashville, 2009

We returned to the scene of our glorious victory four years earlier with a completely different cast of characters. Of the 17 who made the trip in 2005, only Zachary Huey was in 8th grade and therefore a senior in 2009, but he had stopped playing chess.

We were starting all over again with the long-time control and marathon nature of the event. Was the 2005 performance a fluke?

This time we brought 13 players spread over five sections. Unlike in 2005, we were not able to amass six or seven players into one section and give ourselves some depth. This made it less likely we would win anything because if one player had a bad tournament in a given section, it would hurt the team. Remember, the top four scores equal the team score and in some sections, we did not even have four players! We did have some younger players this time though, so we competed in some junior high and elementary sections for the first time. Here was our lineup by section:

K12 U1200
Trent Kannegieter
Kevin Nelson
Wesley Dean

K12 U800 (Changed from U900 at the last Super Nationals)
Scott Dahlke
Blake Nelson
Eric Peterson
Hayden Gunn

K9 Unrated
Will Runels
Peyton Winstead
Rebecca Pober

K6 Unrated
Richard O'Neill

Andrew Smith

<u>K3 U800</u>
Ty Kannegieter

Matt Cazalas was registered for the U1200 section to give us four players there, but he got sick before the event and did not make the trip, leaving us shorthanded. We knew going in that we were not going to defend our U1200 National Title.

Again we shared a team room with another school. Susan Kantor was the sponsor from a school in nearby Tennessee and they only fielded a couple of players, including her son. We treated him like one of our own players and I went over his games between rounds if he wanted. Susan works for the U.S. Chess Federation, now headquartered in Nashville, and it would be difficult to meet a nicer person.

As play began, we learned that our success four years earlier was not a fluke. The Bayside players quickly adjusted to the long time controls and started scoring points. As expected, the U1200 team struggled because they only had three players. They finished with nine of a possible twenty-one points and out of the running, but Kevin turned in a plus score.

The younger players all cashed points: Ty nailed down two, including going undefeated on Sunday. Richard and Andrew each won three games in their section, and one of them was the last player to finish during one of the late night rounds, to include all of the high school students. The K9 unrated team surprised us with a top ten finish! While this was a lighter section with fewer teams than most, it was still impressive for a three-player team to bring home some hardware.

Will scored five points out of seven and took home an individual trophy for 9th place. Peyton had a plus score, and Rebecca was the first girl we brought to a national tournament. I remember Will coming back to the team room after one round with a big grin on his face. "How did you do?" I asked.

"I won." he responded.

"How did it happen? It was hard to see your position, but it looked close."

"I just came up with some good plans." I guess it was that easy. The biggest story of the event was the U800 team.

I walked into the main playing hall before the first round to see former World Champion Gary Kasparov make the ceremonial first move from the stage, as one would see a celebrity throw out the first pitch before a baseball game. Blake's game was located right next to the aisle, so I decided to park myself there for the majority of the round. To my great satisfaction he took a lead and went into the end game with a knight and about three pawns against four pawns.

It should have been a straightforward win, but Blake allowed his opponent to work one pawn too far down the board before he could stop it. The opponent queened the pawn and won the game. It was a heartbreaking kind of loss, and certainly not one you want to absorb in the first round. On the heels of a disappointing season the year before, I was beginning to wonder when and if the light bulb would go on in Blake's head for him to play winning chess. I knew he was capable, and I did not have to wait long for the answer because he won his remaining six games of the tournament!

The team only managed 1.5 points in the first round, but turned in a perfect second, going 4-0. They tallied another three each in rounds three and four and roared back into contention before wavering slightly in round five with two points. They regained their momentum on Sunday morning with three more points and sat in the top five heading into the final round. This was well better than my expectations, to compete for another National Title in our second trip with a small team.

Again, I identified the teams we were chasing. First place belonged to Northwest High of Germantown, Maryland, coached by the able Robert Youngblood. As I have gotten to know him over the years, I consider him the finest scholastic chess coach in the nation because of what he gets out of his students, and it is my privilege to compete against his program.

There is much less pressure on a team when you are chasing down teams in front of you as opposed to trying to hang on to a lead. Recall that four years earlier, we had lost the lead after round six and had to make up ground. My preference from a stress standpoint is to get into first and stay there!

My players greatly impressed me with their stamina for the whole event and finished with a flourish: a perfect 4-0 final round. This put us into contention for first and again it was a waiting game to see how the other teams did. I chased down Coach Youngblood, who kept a crumpled sheet of notebook paper in his back pocket with his hand-written players' names and results. "Coach, how did you do this round?" I asked anxiously.

"I don't know." he shook his head regretfully. "We may have left some points out there. How did you do?"

"We got four points." I beamed.

He winced as if in pain to hear that. "That might be enough."

As it turned out, it wasn't. Northwest finished with 21 points and Bayside and another team finished with 20.5. Ironically, that was how many points we had in 2005 to win it, but this time it was a half point shy. Still, I have never been any prouder of a group of kids I have coached, and their accomplishment is every bit as impressive, in my view, as that of the team that won the National Championship. Collectively, all players again had a plus score and as a team we netted over 500 rating points.

Individual awards followed. Eric finished with five points and earned a trophy because he tied for 20th place overall. Scott Dahlke scored 5.5 points and earned 15th place. Blake, with six wins, took home the 8th place trophy in the section. As for the team, we lost the tiebreak for 2nd place and took home 3rd. By any measure the trip was a phenomenal success. It just is not as well known because we did not take first, and that part is too bad.

Nationals 2010, Columbus, Ohio

The next season opened with a change in our league director. No one was prepared to take his place, so we divided into two divisions: a Mobile Division and a Baldwin Division. One coach from each division stepped up to schedule and direct play, with the idea that the two champions would meet at the end to decide the league title. The Daphne coach, Jonathan Ling, volunteered to conduct the Baldwin side, and he did so well that he took over as league director thereafter, and the two-division format became a one-year experiment.

However, the two divisions served to squash the Baldwin County Tournament as a separate entity because that season we were all playing each other anyway. Again, Bayside fielded such depth and quality that it almost hearkened back to the earlier days of our program when we were just hitting our stride. We were starting to hit it again. That year I counted 29 players who represented us at some point during the season. In addition, Mrs. Kalaris started offering an after-school program to teach the young kids how to play chess. Including her 15-20, that gave us 45-50 kids, making us one of the largest programs at Bayside, including football.

Because of our depth, another interesting feat took place that year. Recall that the previous year our junior high team won the league outright. This year our B team did. As a gesture to our seniors, Kevin, Hayden, Trey, and Sidney Jackson, I put them on the varsity team. And since the league started playing a mixed schedule, meaning A, B, and C teams could all play each other, it did not matter. The B team of Eric, Blake, Scott, and Matt Cazalas, had more than enough firepower to capture the Baldwin Division.

This set up a showdown match with the Mobile champions, ASMS, for the league title. Because we did not all gather at the same place for matches that year, I was unable to scout them and did not know what to expect. I did not need to worry: we steamrolled them 4-0 and collected our sixth title in seven years. Eric Peterson defended the Morphy as a freshman.

Next up was state but there was a conflict: the weekend it was scheduled was the same as part of Bayside's spring break. Also, there was popular demand from the parents to return to Nationals, so it seemed a logistical stretch that year to attend both. Unfortunately, I let personal issues get in the way as well. At state the previous year, the ACF president and vice president assured me that the tournament would be held in southern Alabama the next year. It had not been there since 2001 and we were overdue to host.

But they went back on that promise and held it in northern Alabama again. Not wanting to make two long trips in a short time, we bailed on state and held our own local tournament. We drew some local teams and had fun, but looking back I regret not going to state. Our seniors never earned a ring and it had then been five years since our last state triumph.

Instead, we climbed on a plane for the first time for domestic travel and headed to Columbus, Ohio for the High School Nationals. Because this was not a Super Nationals with all age groups, there was a much smaller turnout: about 1,200 instead of over 5,000. I liked our chances because we could load up and enter 8 players in the U1200 section: Kevin, Blake, Matt, Scott, Wesley, Eric, Hayden, and Peyton. All of them except Matt had Nationals experience and we came so close the year before that I expected to contend.

Simultaneous to this event was the All Girls National held at the same venue. We registered Rebecca Pober to compete in this six-round event, and she held her own, scoring two points. Tradition continued as we shared a team room with a junior high team from Ohio and made some new friends.

The hotel was the best venue for watching games I have ever seen. An escalator took spectators up to a balcony overlooking the playing hall. The walls of the balcony were made of glass and there were chairs for comfortable seating. I could actually sit down and watch the games! My feet were never so happy. Even better, because my players were all playing in the same section, they were relatively close together so I could scan from board to board with my binoculars.

I remember watching Matt play in his first Nationals game in the first round, as he went up against a player from Northwest in Maryland. The game was pretty even, but Matt was way ahead on time. I was starting to mentally count it as a win when he suddenly agreed to a draw. I raced downstairs to accost him coming out of the hall. "What happened?" I demanded.

"It was an even position and there was no way to break through."

"Why didn't you let him run out of time?" I implored.

"I never thought of that." I chalked that up to inexperience and moved on. The rest of the team scored a perfect 4.0 points and we grabbed the fast start I was looking for, just as in 2005.

However, that was completely reversed in the second when we scored none. That was a shock to the system and seemed to knock us out of contention altogether. But I had learned the year before that there is always time to come back. On Saturday the pattern repeated: we roared to 4.0 point in round three and 3.5 in round four, but managed only a half point in round five. It seemed we were running out of gas in the late rounds, which was counter-intuitive to me. Usually I was worried about teenage boys playing well in morning games, but this team was opposite to stereotype.

Round six saw us grab another 4.0 points on Sunday morning, leaving us with 16.0 heading into the final round. I knew we needed about 20.0 to win it, so if we could gain another 4.0 points in round seven, another National Championship would be within grasp. Having that opportunity in a final round is all any chess coach can ask.

We only gained two of four and finished tied for 9th place, which shows the fine line between a great tournament and a championship one: two points separated the top nine teams. It was still an impressive performance as we took our fourth top-ten finish in three Nationals. Kevin and Eric each scored five out of seven and received trophies for finishing tied for 30th. Again we had a plus score as a team and again we netted rating points. They Bayside chess machine rolled on.

Nationals 2011, Nashville, Tennessee

One thunderclap that hit the program at the end of the 2010 season was at the team party: Eric Peterson announced he was going to ASMS for his sophomore year. The two-time defending Morphy champ was not just going to be unavailable for us. He was going to play against us for our mortal enemy.

This time though, there was compensation. A 6th grader moved into our area from Virginia by the name of Steve Chen. This young man already had a 1300 rating, making him the top rated player in our league already. The only problem I foresaw was displacing senior Matt Cazalas on first board for the varsity team, so I had a conversation with him on the first day of practice. "Matt," I began. "We have a new talent on the team."

"Yeah I noticed." he said. "The kid is good."

"He might be good enough to earn first board." I said tentatively. "Is that okay with you?"

"Coach, I just want to win." What an attitude! I wish I had a whole team full of guys like Matt.

The season began, and we continued our winning ways. Steve stubbed his toe and lost against Daphne, which prevented him from winning the Morphy, but his teammates picked him up and carried us to victory. I was attending the birth of our second daughter for the sixth-round showdown against ASMS and had to get my report by phone.

Matt gave me a blow by blow account of how he outmaneuvered a very strong opponent in the end game and pulled out the decisive win as Bayside prevailed 3-1. Another league championship was ours. Even better, the state tournament was finally coming back to southern Alabama for the first time in a decade and Bayside Academy won the bid to host it!

That was the good news. The bad news was that we were not going to be allowed to win it. Here a quick explanation is necessary. Scholastic chess in our state had been growing in popularity over the past few years due to an influx of high-quality coaches like Caesar Lawrence, Balagee Govindan, and Charles Smith. For the most part, these coaches instructed players through private clubs that drew kids from many different schools as opposed to being at one school.

The ACF was pleased to see the increased attendance at chess events around the state, and these coaches served in various capacities for the ACF. It was therefore not surprising that the rules changed to allow club, or all-star teams, to compete with school teams for the state championship. This would be like allowing traveling club soccer or baseball teams to compete against school teams: it was completely unfair.

I argued that no other state in the nation ran their state tournaments in this fashion, and that it was not in line with the USCF rules for teams at Nationals. Only players from the same school may compete on a team there. I campaigned for a separate championship for club teams. While I found an occasional sympathetic ear, it was too late to change the rules for that event: all-star teams would be eligible to win.

On top of that, the state tournament fell on the same weekend as the school musical, and most of my team was in it. In the first round we faced ASMS and I watched Matt lose to

Eric on second board in the most dismal manner as our team lost. Afterward I asked him what was the matter. He replied that he had the songs of "The Music Man" running through his head. It did not matter. Chess Kids Nation, the club team, won the tournament and a long-prized opportunity to host was wasted.

While that result was disgusting, all that remained that season was to pick ourselves up, dust ourselves off, and head up the road to Nashville for the High School Nationals. Getting there was somewhat of an adventure. I drove up with my family and it was difficult to find a hotel room in northern Alabama in the wake of a major tornado that had knocked out power over a wide area. On our way we saw armies of utility trucks heading south on Interstate 65 to lend help.

Once there we fielded 11 players: five on the U1200 team, five one the U800, and Steve who played alone in the open section because of his high rating. He was the first Bayside player to play there, and scored a respectable three out of seven points. Considering his young age and that he was competing against masters and experts, I thought that was pretty good.

This time our team room was cut in half such that we had a section to ourselves, although we were technically sharing it with a team from New York. The dividing wall was thin, and their coach kept wondering what all the racket was about as we roared with approval and applause every time a Bayside player came back with a win.

That tournament I also had the treat of meeting Robby Adamson, coach at Catalina Foothills High in Arizona. His team had won multiple National Titles in the open section and he was featured in *Chess Life* Magazine. In his spare time he is an attorney, and the article mentioned how much he earned for his stipend as coach. I was a little proud to see that my stipend was a little bit higher!

The only exchange we had other than when I congratulated him on all his past success was when I saw him walking back to his team room with a glum look on his face. "What's the matter, coach?" I asked.

"I just had a master lose in the first round." he responded.

"Coach, I cannot relate to your problems."

Both of our teams got off to decent starts, and by the end of the first day, the U800 team was doing better with three points in each of the first two rounds. I took a break to take my six-year-old daughter for dinner and as we were standing in line to place our order, she lost her first tooth. That night she wrote a note to the Tooth Fairy and left in on the window sill of our room: "Dear Tooth Fairy," it began. "I am staying in Nashville now." She did not want her monetary award to be misplaced.

The second day the tide turned some, and the U1200 team surpassed the U800. Both were in contention for top-ten finishes and both were paced by a Cazalas sibling. On the U1200 team, senior Matt was leading the way and ended with 5.5 out of 7.0 and a trophy for tying for 9th overall. Meanwhile, no one in the U800 section could handle his sister, Marissa. She came back with win after win, telling us what different tactic she used to score the victory. She also scored 5.5 and tied for 11th place, taking home the 14th place trophy.

The cheering from her teammates every time she came back with a win even disrupted the team in the next room!

For those who understand chess, one of her wins was truly amazing and amusing. She had the lead in the end game and one of her pawns reached the other side of the board for promotion. Instead of getting a queen though, she got a bishop. "Why did you get a bishop?" I queried.

"Because if I got a queen, my opponent would take it."

"But you had the queening square covered. If your opponent took the queen with his last remaining big piece, you would capture back and have an easy win."

"I didn't want to lose my queen." Then she wound up checkmating her opponent with two bishops: very difficult to do, especially under the stress of a major tournament, and the only time in all my years of coaching that any of my players has done that.

The U800 team finished with 16 points, good enough for a 12th place trophy. The U1200 finished with three points in the final round for a total of 18. That was the same score we had the previous year, and this time is was good for a tie for 5th. We took home the 8th place trophy, but it was our third top-five finish, and fifth top-ten in four Nationals. Once again, we had a plus score and netted nearly 700 rating points from the rest of the country. It was a great way to end the season.

Nationals 2012, Minneapolis, Minnesota

We were loaded again for the 2012 season, but somewhat senior-heavy. Blake, Scott, and Peyton all returned for their senior years and were joined for varsity consideration by junior Wesley and 7th graders Steve and Trent. My natural inclination is to move away from reliance on seniors if at all possible. I prefer to develop younger talent in players who will be with the program for a longer time.

I therefore had my eye on Trent for fourth board to join Steve, Blake and Wesley. Trent was coming off an outstanding 6th grade campaign where he won the trophy for best player under 8th grade in our league and I thought he was ready for more of a challenge on varsity. However, he was resistant to the idea. His view was that playing first board, even on a lower team, was better because he was taking on the best player of that team. I overruled him as coach, but I always prefer it when the player and I are on the same page.

As the season opened, we had to play ASMS in the second round. We narrowly took care of business 3-1 with my preferred lineup, but Eric beat Blake on board two to make it close. Our former player was still a thorn in our side. We cruised from there to our eighth league title and Steve Chen won the Morphy. The next stop was Bessemer, Alabama for the state tournament.

Trent was unavailable for the tournament because he had a conflict as a top tennis player for Bayside, and tennis is a spring sport. Had he been there, I very likely would have played him on the junior high team along with Marissa and fellow 7th grader Harrison Costantini who came on very strong that year. In fact, Harrison had beaten Trent in a league match that year and with a fully loaded team like that, we would have had a legitimate shot at a double State Championship. As it was, the short-handed junior high team took 2nd place, our highest finish in that division since 2004.

For the varsity, we still had the very capable Scott Dahlke, who was part of the 2nd place finish at Nationals as a freshman. I assigned Peyton to platoon with Scott on fourth board. Happily, we reached a partially satisfying solution with the ACF about the format. The good news was that all-star club teams would have a separate championship. The bad news was that because there were so few of them, they would be combined with the scholastic teams in the same section and their games against scholastic teams would count in the standings. In other words, the club teams would still affect the outcome of the scholastic championship.

It was still better than conditions the previous year when none of the scholastic teams had a chance, so I went with it. The morning of the team event, I woke up in my hotel room and went downstairs for breakfast where I was greeted by the ASMS team. "Great," I thought. "Didn't we already beat these guys once?" The shark tank in which we were competing just got tougher.

The location was also not a neutral site. As I walked around the facility, I saw an office for Coach Smith, the Indian Springs coach, complete with photos and chess trophies. Apparently, he used the place to teach some of his students and Bessemer is not that far from the Indian Springs campus.

Sure enough, we drew ASMS as our opponent in the first round, but we had been preparing hard. This time we dispatched them 4-0 and Blake crushed Eric. Comment soverheard afterward from Eric were, "Wow, Blake is awesome!" and "Why did we even come up here?" Not to be uncharitable, but those were exactly the thoughts I wanted their team to think!

Chess Kids Nation defeated Indian Springs in the first round and we had to play them in the second where we lost by the narrowest of scores: 1-2-1. Next, we played another club team from Huntsville and defeated them 3-1, although Steve lost on first board. Finally, we faced Indian Springs for all the scholastic championship marbles: each of us had one loss, so our final match would decide it.

I felt confident going in because I truly felt we had the better team, so imagine my dismay when, after Steve won his game, Blake and Scott both went down to defeat. Now it was all on Wesley to win just to hold the draw and share a State Title, but a quick glance at his board indicated he was losing badly. To say I was in shock and disbelief is an understatement.

To the parents and other players peering into the playing hall to get a read on how the game was going, I'm sure that my body language was not encouraging. I slumped down into a chair behind Wesley. My head drooped. I even spit out my gum. Anyone who knows me in regard to coaching recognizes that I chomp gum like crazy during any big match, so spitting it out is the equivalent of waving the white flag.

The sanitized version of the thoughts going through my head at the time were woesome. "We worked so hard this year, and it is all for naught. We have to wait a whole other year to get back to this position and try again. Our seniors are not going to go out with a ring. What more could I have done as coach?"

Suddenly my morose mental fog was pierced by a question. Wesley was raising his hand to ask the tournament director a question. "What is your question?" asked the director.

"I'd like to ask my coach if I can accept a draw." My jaw almost hit the floor. In twelve years of coaching, no player had ever taken the opportunity to ask me this, although it was perfectly legal and I had briefed my players about it. I guess I was amazed to see it actually happen!

"Go ahead." said the director.

Wesley looked up at me and I responded as decisively as I could, "Play on." I realized he might not be aware of his teammates' results and a draw only would have cemented our loss as a team by a score of 1-2-1. We needed him to win, however unlikely, to make it a 2-2 tie. Wesley obediently turned around to play his hopeless position.

Meanwhile our nervous senior captain, Blake, was coming in and out of the room to check on Wesley's game and report back to the rest of the team. I mentioned before that Blake and Wesley were at each other's throats at practice as younger players, aggravating me to no end. But as they grew older and matured, they became friends. The irony at that moment was that Blake's fate rested entirely in Wesley's hand.

I have to explain a little about chess to describe how Wesley's game finished. No good record of it exists because Wesley stopped taking notation due to time trouble. The only pieces he had left were a king, a rook, and two pawns. His opponent had a king, bishop, knight, rook, and at least one pawn, which was one square away from queening. Wesley could have stopped it, but only at the cost of his rook which would leave him with no chance at all. The only redeeming feature of his position was that the opposing king was in the corner and Wesley had worked his two connected pawns down to the sixth rank facing the king.

If Wesley could sneak his rook to the back rank, he could get a checkmate, which in this case would be the equivalent of a Hail Mary pass at the end of a football game. You would not want to hang by the odds. His opponent did not have to queen his pawn, but he did, and crucially did not put Wesley in check by doing so. That gave Wesley the miraculous opportunity he needed, and he calmly slid his rook to the other side of the board. "Checkmate." he said, extending his hand in a show of sportsmanship.

Just before the move, I'm sure my eyes bugged out in disbelief. Blake raced out of the room to spread the word: after a seven-year drought that felt more like 70 to me, Bayside Academy was State Champions! With the tie, it was a co-championship, and I congratulated Coach Smith. In his shock at the sudden outcome, all he could do was sputter about not being happy with a shared title, and berate his player for letting that one get away.

To top it off, we won the tiebreaker for the first-place trophy. We had more board wins and a better record against common opponents in the event than Indian Springs. I had to pinch myself to make sure it was not a dream and the four-hour drive home by myself was a breeze. All that remained was to go to Nationals.

The parents really were the driving force behind going to Nationals for four consecutive years. The same core of them went to all four, and while their kids were battling out on the chess board, they all went out on the town and had fun! I saw a few incriminating photos, one of in which they were all dressed in cowboy type outfits.

This time we got on a plane to Minneapolis and shared a team room with Sparta High from New Jersey, coached by Tom Murray. That might have been the most fun I had sharing such a room because Tom and I had much in common: we both are professional investment advisors, we each drove the same type of car, and we love coaching our kids in chess.

Only five players made the trip, all in the U1200 section: Blake, Wesley, Scott, Peyton, and Marissa. We started well on Friday, leveled out some on Saturday, and finished strong on Sunday with 6.5 out of 8.0 points. This left us with a grand total of 19.0, one better than the previous two years, and outright possession of 5th place. The nice thing about a top-five finish at Nationals is that the top five players on the team each get a plaque.

Individual honors came as well. Blake scored 5.5 out of 7.0, a fine way to finish his Bayside career, and tied for 13th overall, taking home the 21st place trophy. Wesley was even more impressive. He turned in an undefeated effort, going 5-0-2, for a total of six points and matching Stephen Smith's landmark record from seven years earlier. This earned him a tie for 2nd overall, and he took home the 4th place trophy on tiebreaks.

Testament to Wesley came from the coach of the winning team: Abington High of Pennsylvania. Wesley defeated one of their players in the sixth round, and I was talking to the coach during the seventh to see if there was an outside chance we could catch them. "Is Dean one of yours?" he asked.

"Yes." I said proudly.

"He's good. We don't want to play him anymore." he replied, shaking his head. In fact, no one could beat Wesley in the entire season. His overall record was 15-0-3. One of the three draws came against an all-star player at state and the other two were at Nationals. Oh, and he was only a junior!

As I took stock of the team in the off season, despite the loss of three dear seniors, our future looked extremely bright. With Steve coming back as an 8th grader and Wesley on board two, we had the best one-two punch in the state of Alabama. Then we had rising sophomore Marissa with two national tournaments under her belt, and powerhouse 8th graders Trent and Harrison.

What did I possibly have about which to worry?

In battle. Matt Cazalas ponders a move during High School Nationals in Columbus, Ohio, 2010. While Matt was not on a State Championship team as a player, he came back after graduation to help me coach and earned a ring for helping the 2015 team capture the title. As Senior Captain, he unselfishly gave up playing first board for a more talented sixth grader. That is an example of a team player.

High School Nationals 2012 from Minneapolis, Minnesota. Bayside Academy finished 5th in the U1200 section. L-r: Blake Nelson, Scott Dahlke, Peyton Winstead, Wesley Dean, Coach Eric Nager, Marissa Cazalas. Wesley and Blake are holding individual trophies they won at the same event.

Chapter 9

MORE OBSTACLES

Unsustainable Losses

I had plenty about which to worry when the 2013 season began. A confluence of independent events served to devastate our program. Marissa left Bayside because they did not have an extensive marching band program. Trent decided to take a year off from chess and focus on tennis. Harrison's parents went through a painful divorce that took him and his siblings away from Bayside. Overnight our depth went from a strength to a liability.

This forced me to promote players to the varsity level that needed more seasoning at the junior varsity level. I pressed freshman Philip Dobbins and 7th grader Andrew Smith into service. Both were good players, and both had experience at Nationals, but they were not quite yet ready for varsity in my opinion. Below them we had between four and six 6th and 4th graders who were playing their first or second year of chess and that was it. Those ten players were the entire program.

I appealed to the new headmaster for help in recruiting. Mr. Johnson retired after many years and a younger man who had grown up in Canada took his place. This encouraged me at first because chess is taught in the schools there nationally. But he quickly disappointed me after our first conversation. "I need some help recruiting for our program." I started.

"Yeah, there are so many activities out there for the kids." he replied.

"We have had such success as a program, I think it should be a point of emphasis for the school."

"The kids are going to have to choose from themselves what they want to be involved in." He was going to be no help.

On top of this, at the first match I was greeted with the demoralizing scene of Marissa and the Costantini brothers filling the top three spots on Daphne's team. Fortunately, our strength at the top of our lineup got us through the first four rounds undefeated, and then the December matches loomed. As Mr. Ling took over the league, we went from one match per month with a game in sixty-minute time control to two matches per month at game in thirty. This allowed for coordinating transportation for fewer league meetings and for players to play more than one game in a month. While I understood his reasoning, I still did not like the shorter time control.

Our first opponent that month was UMS-Wright. And who was their first-year coach, but my brother, Paul. He had relocated to the area the previous year for work, and the summer before school started he attended a high school reunion. At the reunion was a classmate who happened to be the principal at

UMS. Paul asked for the job as chess coach and was hired on the spot. UMS has a long, successful chess tradition, winning our league the first two years it existed and capturing a state title in the 1980s. But their program was dropped when a faculty sponsor left, and Paul revived it.

He had read my book and was at a bigger school than Bayside with many smart kids to choose from, so I knew they would be a formidable opponent. He also had at least one player with league experience from when their program participated in the league a couple of years before. I was about 15 minutes away from leaving my office for the match when I got a phone call from second board Wesley: "Coach, I don't know if I can make the match today."

"Why not?" I asked. "Is everything okay?"

"My friend is really sick and I'm going to see him in the hospital." While I had great compassion for Wesley and his friend, this placed our team in a real pickle.

Wesley held out hope that he could make it back before the match ended, so I had no choice but to leave his position open and let his opponent start Wesley's clock. He never made it back and his clock ran out, meaning we lost that board by forfeit. UMS beat us on the lower two boards and won the match. I was more upset about the circumstances than the loss and I am sure that is not how Paul wanted to win. Still, he was temporarily the only coach in the league with a winning record against Bayside!

We managed to win our next two matches which put us back into contention for a final round battle against ASMS. Steve won his game and clinched the Morphy again as an 8th grader. But for the first time in over two years, Wesley lost. In fairness to him, his heart was not into chess his senior year, and I'm sure his friend's illness had something to do with that. (Good news: his friend had a complete recovery and his younger brother now plays on our team!) The team lost and we settled for 3rd place.

I could tell then that I was not going to take our team to state, and for a fleeting moment I considered putting together an all-star team of Steve, Wesley, senior Eric Peterson from ASMS, and Michael Tran to compete at state instead. I asked these players about that possibility at the final round, but Eric spoke for them in putting the idea to a quick end: "We're done playing chess." I did not take that to mean never playing the game again, but as seniors with big life transitions close at hand, they wanted to place their focus elsewhere.

One bright spot at state was that Steve played in the individual tournament and won the title as Middle School State Champion: Bayside's first outright individual champ. This entitled him to play in the Barber Tournament of middle school champions from around the country where he represented Alabama. Run in conjunction with the U.S. Open, it is a big deal and a big honor.

Overall though, it was a disappointing season and not a worthy end for a player of Wesley's caliber who finished his career #2 on the all-time Bayside wins list. Our four-year reign at the top of the league ended and it showed the downside of being at a small school. Losing just a few players made a huge difference. Only the next season offered hope of consolation.

A Recruiting Plea Answered

The 2014 season opened with even more uncertainty. Thankfully, Trent Kannegieter came back to the program for his freshman year. He and Steve were classmates and buddies, and I'm sure that helped encourage him to return. This gave us a lethal 1-2 punch at the top of the lineup again, because if Trent played for any other team in our league, he would be a solid first board. Philip came back as a sophomore, and this time he was ready for varsity play. One of the few bright spots of the previous season was that Philip had won first place in the scholastic division of our annual tournament, the Bayside Open. All we lacked was a fourth board.

No new kids came out to the first practice so I had to recruit. I asked the school for help again, and this time they said if I wrote something up, they would circulate it for me. So I made something like a David Letterman Top Ten List of why you should be on the chess team. The reasons ranged from looking good on a high school transcript, to our long tradition of winning, to the simple appeal of having fun with your friends.

I held my breath and waited. At the next practice, exactly one new player showed up: senior Keegan Cort. I was disappointed on two counts: first, only one player? Second, a senior? He could only help us for one year. What good was that? Upon further reflection, I decided to count my blessings. The alternative was to promote a 6th grader with one year of experience to the varsity, and that was not an option.

As I began to work with him, I saw that Keegan had some experience with chess and he was teachable. One of the basic end game lessons I teach is how to hold a draw with only a king against a king and pawn. Keegan showed his mettle early in a third-round match against ASMS, using the technique I showed him to earn the draw. Thanks to him, we won the match 2-1-1. The next month we took out Fairhope and UMS to clinch the league title.

Steve did not win the Morphy that year. I perceived that a couple of teams in our league were stacking their boards against us, such that their best player was not playing first board. There is no specific rule against this in our unrated league but I still did not like it. So in those cases, I played Steve on second board against who I knew to be the opposing team's best. The main instance of this came against Fairhope where Michael Tran deferred to a senior teammate and let him play first. Steve and Michael battled to a draw on second board. The Fairhope senior ended up with the Morphy.

Much more ominously, I got wind early in the school year that Steve was thinking seriously about attending ASMS for his sophomore year. Losing a player of his caliber would be too much to take, so I went straight to the administration. "What is your plan for retaining Steve Chen?" I asked.

"Oh, is he thinking of leaving?" replied an administrator coolly.

"Yes. He is a great asset to the school as a student, not just a chess player."

"Why would he not be happy at Bayside?" Ugh. It was not a question of him not being happy at Bayside! He was. But he thought that he might have better opportunity elsewhere. I had to take matters into my own hands.

In December I invited Steve's parents to my office on a weekend for a meeting. His dad came and we had a nice, heart to heart conversation. "I do not want Steve to leave." I told him earnestly.

"Steve likes playing for you. That would be the toughest part of leaving." his dad replied, whose name is Tao.

"I can write letters of recommendation for him. He is a great kid and I would not hesitate to give him the highest endorsement. What else can I do?"

"He is very competitive. He likes to play first board and compete for the Morphy." It had not occurred to me that not playing him first could affect his desire to stay.

"I promise to play him first board for the rest of his time at Bayside." This was not a very bold promise on my part. By then Steve was at least 500 rating points better than anyone else on the team. Unless some miracle took place that a higher rated player moved to Bayside, I was confident Steve would remain in the top position. And if someone else did move in, I would cross that bridge then!

Steve did stay, and I do not believe it was because of my pledge. Instead, I think it was because I showed how much I cared and made the extra effort to reach out to the family. I had just completed my most successful recruiting mission as Bayside Chess Coach: retaining Steve.

One more word on this remarkable player – many players of his ability might not be interested in playing in our scholastic chess league. They might view it as beneath them. But Steve is a team player. He loves his teammates, works with them patiently in practice, and encourages them. Because of his years of sustained excellence, he is, in my opinion, the greatest player ever to compete in the Mobile-Baldwin County Chess League.

State Tournament, 2014

The geographic center of Alabama is Montgomery, the state capitol. It is no more than a three-hour drive from anywhere in the state. Despite its central location, not much scholastic chess is played there. Still, it would make sense to have state tournaments there for travel purposes: teams or individuals could drive there in the morning and be home the same night, avoiding the expense of overnight stays.

The ACF saw things differently. To them, Birmingham is "central," even though it is 90 minutes north of Montgomery and over a four-hour drive for those of us in the southern part of the state. That year we were off to the campus of Montevallo University, about 30 minutes south of Birmingham, for the state championships.

Our preparation was shaky. While Keegan helped us greatly during the regular season, he kind of marched to his own drummer. He did not always show up at practice. I could not get mad at him, because we would not have a varsity team without him. For the first time as a coach, a player had significant leverage over me.

Prior to state I called a mandatory practice on campus on a Saturday to prepare specifically for the teams we would face. Keegan did not show. I seriously considered booting him off the team at that point. When I cooled down, I realized it would not do any good to the team to do so. On the other hand, how could we be expected to win as a team if he was not prepared?

We made the trip and play began. The first round opened against Covenant Christian, a relative newcomer to chess who I thought we could handle without too much trouble. The result was a 2-2 draw, with Steve and Trent winning and Keegan and Philip losing. That was not the way a prospective State Champion opens a tournament.

In the second round we faced Paul's UMS team with the same results as the first round from the same players: another 2-2 draw. I remember passing a note to Paul during the match stating that if we tied each other, it would probably destroy each of our chances to win it. His team also drew in the first round, and a second draw gave us each the equivalent of one win and one loss halfway through the event. Meanwhile, Indian Springs won both of their first two matches. It was not looking good.

That year there was yet another all-star team mucking about in our division: a team from Caesar Chess who only fielded three players. In each match they forfeited the fourth board game. They had drawn UMS in the first round, and in the third they played Indian Springs. Much to my surprise, Indian Springs lost, despite a free win on board four. That opened the door for the rest of us. Maybe club teams had their uses after all.

Paul brought two teams to the event, and in round three we played his B team. We finally got on track by blasting them 4-0, which lifted us into a three-way tie for first place with Indian Springs and UMS A with one round left to play. It was a three-way tie because also in the third round, UMS A struggled mightily but slipped past Fairhope for a win.

The final round pairings stood to be Bayside vs. Caesar Chess and UMS vs. Indian Springs. But there were an odd number of teams in the event, so one team received a bye each round. As I was walking on campus not long before the final round began, an idea struck me: why not have only the scholastic teams decide the scholastic team championship? Caesar Chess could get the bye! I raced to the tournament director's office. "Let's give the club team the bye." I said breathlessly.

"Why, what do you mean?" he inquired.

"Let's allow the scholastic teams to play it out for the title without interference from a club team."

"I'll take it under advisement." he said hopefully. "It is a legal pairing." When the pairings were posted, they read UMS vs. Covenant Christian and Bayside vs. Indian Springs. It would be scholastic vs. scholastic and if we won, we'd be State Champions. I almost fainted: someone from the ACF had listened to me.

The games began, and Steve wrecked his opponent on first board in short order. Philip went down to defeat on fourth board leaving Trent and Keegan to carry the fight. As I was watching, I kept an eye on UMS. They prevailed in their match, clinching at least a share of the title. The pressure was on us.

Two years before, Wesley Dean was the first Bayside player in 12 years of coaching ever to ask me if he should accept a draw. In the 2014 tournament, it happened with both Keegan and Trent in the final round! Keegan asked first. By then the process was more refined. The tournament director escorted me outside the playing room and asked for my answer that he would relay to my player. I could only answer in one of two prescribed ways: "A draw will help us," or "a draw will not help us."

Trent was ahead slightly in his game, so I said a draw would help us. Keegan, who had a nice position of his own, executed one of the most brilliant sacrifices and series of exchanges to get to the point where he had a pawn and king against a knight and king. While he was down in material, he maneuvered himself into a position where he could not lose. It is impossible to force checkmate with a king and knight. At worst it would be a draw.

Then Trent's opponent asked him for a draw out of desperation. A draw on second board would have drawn the match so I said, "A draw will NOT help us." Trent politely declined and finished demolishing his opponent in the end game, after which he gave me one of the biggest bear hugs I ever received. Bayside was State Champions. Keegan's game continued, but I did not see the end of it because I was tossed out of the room for being too giddy.

He actually ended up queening his pawn and winning, which turned out to be significant as we went into a tiebreak procedure with UMS. Just as in 2012, total board wins and strength of competition, in part measured by how many opponents had byes, would determine it. Bayside played two teams with byes while UMS played three so our schedule was deemed tougher. And, by virtue of our 4-0 win in round three over the UMS B team, we also had more board wins. Bayside captured the first-place trophy.

Still it was pretty cool to share a State Championship with my brother. In only his second year of coaching he had won it, just as I had back in 2002. We had never heard of brothers sharing a title like that, so we submitted photos to the USCF and ACF for publication. We had roomed together in the hotel and we rode back home together in my car, stopping to share a pleasant meal and recount the events of the day.

The surprising turn of events was very humbling because I had virtually nothing to do with Keegan's success. He did it all on his own. What a gift to our program he was. He only played 11 games for us in his entire career but in my mind, he is in the fictitious Bayside Academy Chess Hall of Fame along with all the other great players that went before him. Thank you, Keegan, for answering the call.

As for Trent, I had a burning question for him. He had won a State Championship as a tennis player, so I had to ask, "How did it feel winning at chess compared to tennis?"

"Exactly the same." he beamed.

A Coaching Feat

The next season opened with three returning starters from a State Championship team, so expectations were high. We desperately needed more depth, though. I was not about to go through another season like 2013 and 2014 where missing one player meant a forfeit loss.

Changes came to Bayside at the same time. The young headmaster who replaced Mr. Johnson did not work out, so the board brought in an interim while the search committee went back to work. I decided to act boldly early in the school year and made an appointment with the interim, Mr. Costello. I strode into his office and plunked the National Championship trophy on the floor. "Have you met Coach Schilling?" I began. Coach Ann Schilling is the super star volleyball coach at Bayside who, as of 2016, had won 14 consecutive 2A and 3A State Championships.

"Of course." he responded.

"Good." I said. "Then you already know about the second most successful program at Bayside. I am here to tell you about the most successful." As it turned out, my sales pitch was unnecessary. Mr. Costello served as headmaster at schools in other states with chess programs and was quite familiar with the benefits of the game.

With a more pro-chess administration, I could recruit more effectively. Instead of circulating a memo, I attended Club Day. This is an event early in the school year where the various clubs come together and share what they have to offer with prospective members. At our table we had a couple of the State Championship trophies, and I updated the handout that served to recruit Keegan the year before. The response was tremendous: at least six upper school players came out for the team, as well as some younger kids. A former player, junior Richard O'Neill, came back to play after taking some years off. We could field B and C teams again!

Now my challenge was to determine playing order, especially who was going to play fourth board on varsity. I played a simultaneous with the new players at an early practice, and one of them stood out to me right away – freshman Ford

Taylor. He clearly secured the fourth spot by the time of the first matches. As a coach, that is exactly what you want to happen as opposed to making a difficult judgment call.

We won our first two matches and Ford won both of his games. The lower divisions featured a series of clashes between us and UMS. By his third year, Paul had built a deep program of experienced players and challenged for championships at all levels. Because of this our first-round results were all the more encouraging: our B team tied UMS, and our C team and K-8 team defeated them.

Soon after, UMS held a rated tournament on their campus and some of my players went. It was there that another new Bayside player caught my attention. Freshman Thomas Denton, who played C team first board, defeated a player from the UMS varsity. Immediately I promoted him to B team first board where he could challenge for varsity. An added bonus of having Thomas on the team was his dad, Wade, also a strong player who scrimmaged with the team.

By then Cynthia Klimjack stepped into the position of Team Mom. Her two sons, David and Michael, paced the K-8 teams, and as the season progressed it soon appeared we were in great shape to sweep the titles for all three league divisions. Indeed, the K-8 team finished undefeated with two draws and tied for first with UMS, which had one loss – to us. By virtue of the head-to-head win, we took the first-place trophy. The JV team took clear first, again over UMS. And the varsity, while drawing against UMS in the final round, clinched Bayside's second consecutive title and tenth in twelve years. UMS tied with ASMS for second and won the tiebreak.

In each division that year it was Bayside and UMS 1-2, just as it was at state the previous year. I realize that might not have set well with brother Paul, but he nonetheless should be thrilled at such a phenomenal accomplishment in only his third year of coaching. We would clash yet some more at the state tournament just around the corner, but this year it was in our back yard.

The ACF finally agreed to put southern Alabama on a three-year rotation so that every third year they would hold the state tournament in our area. Bayside bid to host it, and I am glad to say lost the bid to ASMS. I was glad because it is a tremendous amount of work to hold a big event like that, lining up volunteers, concessions, and the logistics of securing buildings, tables, and chairs. At ASMS, they could do all that work and it was a short drive across Mobile Bay for us to compete. All we had to do was show up!

The even better news was that for the first time in several years, the varsity championship would be determined only by scholastic teams. The tournament director took the two club entrants that year and paired them individually against each other. In other words, each team had four players and in each of the four rounds of the tournament, one player from one team would play one player from the other team in a round robin. That way they would not play any scholastic teams and affect the standings, which was never fair to begin with.

Yet another nice aspect of this tournament was for the first time there was a junior varsity team section. I could enter another team to compete for a State Championship, and we could avoid the potential conflict of interest of having an A team and a B team from the same school play each other in the varsity section. We also entered teams in the junior high and elementary divisions. At the varsity level, I judged that Thomas has surpassed Philip, and placed him on fourth board. Philip captained the JV team and took the move with poise and grace.

The games began, and a pretty tough field showed up, featuring the usual suspects from around the state. We opened against John Carroll with a decisive win. Even though their coach had moved on to coach at the elementary level, I relished the chance to have another shot at an old rival. At the same time UMS defeated Indian Springs, which I considered to be a mild upset.

Next up came UMS and a rematch of co-State Champions. In the regular season they had drawn us by playing somewhat out of order, but state required them to play their lineup by strength according to rating. With Steve Chen as our first board, this rule benefited us and we won, although narrowly, by a count of 2-1-1. After falling behind, Thomas rallied for a draw on fourth board. I am sure Paul would say that his guy should have won the game. On the other hand, Ford fumbled away a sure win on board three so in my estimation, the score could very easily have been 3-1 our way. Either way, the better team prevailed.

Indian Springs brought a formidable team and fought us to a draw in round three, scoring a surprising win over Trent on board two. Because of their loss in the first round, they were all but eliminated from the title chase. But with the tie, we left the door open for teams chasing us to catch up.

For the final round it was Bayside vs. ASMS for all the marbles. They had suffered a loss in round two and needed to beat us to secure first. If we tied, UMS could catch us if they won their final round. The best course of action was just to take care of business for ourselves, and this is just what we did. We blasted them 3-0-1, with only Thomas drawing. I was very happy for Ford, who had struggled all day and broke through with a critical win in the final round. As it turned out, UMS drew John Carroll and tied with Indian Springs for second.

The JV team swept their division, consisting of two UMS teams and a home school team. For the third time in Bayside history, we were double State Champions. At the varsity level, it was our sixth championship and for me, the sweetest for several reasons: 1) It took place on the campus of our arch enemy, ASMS, and we beat them in the final round. 2) It was a clear championship, not a co-championship. We won the varsity division by a full point which, in chess, is very decisive. 3) It was a well-run tournament, without the controversy or poor directing we had endured in the past. 4) We did it with our youngest team ever. The varsity consisted of two sophomores and two freshmen, so we stood to be good for a while.

Another measurement showed how far I had come as a coach. One of the achievements of that year of which I am most proud is how quickly we developed new talent. Of the eight players who competed that day on our two State Championship teams, four of them had never played serious competitive chess before that season.

By now, you are probably used to the theme that when the chips seem down for our program, we have some surprising, rapid success. And when we are doing well, some obstacle is thrown in our way. An example of the latter came that summer when I was on vacation with my family. I received a call from Thomas's dad, Wade. I knew that Thomas had looked at applying to ASMS that year, but he was not accepted. He was wait-listed. Wade called to tell me that Thomas had been accepted after all and would attend ASMS in the fall. In the immortal words of Lou Holtz, the former football coach, after hearing the news, I slept like a baby that night: I woke up every two hours and cried.

Sure enough, the loss of Thomas from our team and his addition to ASMS made them our equal for the 2016 season. They tied us in the final round of our regular season and we had to beat them in a speed game playoff (clocks with five minutes per side) to secure the league championship. And without Thomas, Indian Springs wrestled the State Championship away from us in March.

Undaunted, Bayside loaded up for one last run in 2017 with our seniors, Steve and Trent. We defeated ASMS in the season opener but stumbled to a draw against Daphne. This left us in the awkward position of needing ASMS to beat (or tie) Daphne in the final round, which they did, for us to win the league outright again. Steve Chen finished his career with five Morphy Awards.

An incident in the opening round led to an interesting conversation with Jonathan Ling, the Daphne coach. He took offense at a comment I made suggesting that one of his players should come to Bayside, so I invited him to come to my office and clear the air. "Jonathan," I began, "I do appreciate all you do for our league and I hope you know that."

"Yes, and I have to remember that you have a different model at Bayside, where you are an outside coach who is brought in as opposed to a faculty member who does other things besides chess." he replied.

"Well despite that I've never been able to recruit a kid to Bayside just for chess. There are always other factors, like the expense of a private school or activities like sports that have higher priority."

"That is understandable."

"Yet I've lost students to Daphne who participate in other activities, like marching band, for example. If a kid is passionate about that, she should be at Daphne over Bayside because you have a better program. But if the kid is passionate about chess, he should come to Bayside because we give them more opportunity."

"I can't argue with that."

From there we left on good terms. After all, most teams in our league do not attend the state tournament or play rated games. As a good will gesture, we agreed to an annual event at Daphne City Hall to decide the city championship in chess called the Mayor's Cup. The inaugural one was a rematch of our regular season tie, and this time Bayside prevailed.

One bonus during this season was playing in our first ever K-12 Nationals. This is an annual December event that we never attended before because of proximity to the holidays and first semester final exams. This year, however, if fell after exams so we decided to go for it. On top of that, it was in Nashville instead of its usual Florida location, so we could catch the juniors coming back from their annual class trip to Kentucky.

A grade championship differs from a class championship in that you only play opponents in your grade, regardless of rating. This sets up much larger rating disparities than we are used to and our scores showed it. Only one in ten players who made the trip had a plus score. But junior Parker Watts did chop down a redwood, defeating a kid from New York who was rated 900 points higher than he was. And 5th grader Michael Klimjack won first place under 600 rating, a form of a National Title in its own right. I credit this tournament for toughening us for the second half of the season.

At state that year we ended as co-champions with Indian Springs, a good way for the seniors to go out. Steve and Trent finished #1 and #2 all time in wins in Bayside chess history.

I do not want to think about what it will take to replace them, but I do have some other ideas.

Vision for the Future

Bayside Academy is a top-notch college preparatory school in our area, yet it does not exist in a vacuum. There is much competition, ranging from the new Catholic high school in our county, to the International Baccalaureate programs at the two closest high schools. This is not to mention the high-quality private schools across the bay in Mobile, as well as the Alabama School of Math and Science that boasts free tuition.

Bayside needs to leverage its advantages to keep attracting quality students, and chess is one big advantage that Bayside has yet to leverage. Chess is associated with being smart, and that is certainly an image any college prep school should want to cultivate. The list of universities where Bayside chess players have gone speaks for itself.

In my view, there are two things we could do to attract chess players. The first is more travel, both international and domestic. The school could identify a revenue stream from some existing fund-raising sources, like our golf tournament, to help our club augment what we get from our annual rated tournament. These proceeds could be used to subsidize travel every other year.

My first preference for international travel would be to a Spanish speaking country because most Bayside students take Spanish. We could include a Spanish teacher as well as a soccer coach to help make the experience richer and incent more kids to play chess. In the years we did not go abroad, we could host international students at Bayside. The students could stay with Bayside families and attend classes, adding enrichment and cultural perspectives while perhaps playing a match in front of the student body.

For domestic travel, we could go somewhere like Colorado during spring break and play games against my friend Billy Willson's team at Regis Jesuit in between time on the ski slopes. Of course, they would be welcome to visit us the following year around Mardi Gras time and experience the wonders of the Gulf beaches and Southern hospitality.

The second thing is to endow some form of chess scholarship at Bayside. If chess becomes a point of emphasis, and why not with the success we have enjoyed, we could lower the tuition barrier that keeps many students from ever applying in the first place.

It is fun to dream, isn't it?

Coaching my own daughter. My daughter Nicole now plays for Bayside Academy, the biggest privilege of my coaching career.

Co-champions. In 2013 my brother Paul started coaching at
UMS-Wright in Mobile, Alabama. In 2014 our teams tied
for the High School Team State Championship in
Montevallo, Alabama. Here we are holding our
trophies. Bayside Academy won the tiebreaker for the first-
place trophy. It's the first known instance of brother
coaches sharing a chess title.

League Rivals. Here Bayside Academy (left) faces off against UMS – Wright in Junior Varsity action from our 2016 regular season at Trojan Hall on the campus of Daphne High School. Our entire league comes together to one location for our monthly matches. At first board for Bayside is Philip Dobbins.

Varsity Showdown. From the 2016 regular season, Bayside Academy (right) takes on Davidson High School coached by Jeff Knighton. Bayside players from R-L: Steve Chen (first board), Trent Kannegieter, Ford Taylor, Ian Austill. Bayside won the Mobile-Baldwin County Chess League that year for the third consecutive year and eleven of the previous thirteen.

Chapter Ten

LESSONS LEARNED AND RESOURCES

Beyond the competitive aspects, chess is good for school children in a variety of ways. It teaches them such things as analytical thinking, pattern recognition, time management, logic, problem solving skills, good sportsmanship, and immediate consequences for one's actions. Studying chess in a disciplined way forms good study habits, and playing chess is applied mathematics.

If you have ever seen a tournament chess board, you will notice it is a grid eight squares wide by eight squares long. Typically across the bottom, the board is lettered A-H, and numbered along the side 1-8. Those who play chess competitively record their moves as they make them. As an example, with the white pieces, a first move with a knight might be depicted as b1-c3. Whether the player realizes it or not, he has just plotted coordinates on a grid. This is applied algebra. Anecdotal evidence suggests that those who play chess have higher standardized test scores in math and reading subjects than those who do not play. Thirty countries around the world teach chess as a math subject in school.

Chess also looks good on a high school transcript when you are applying to college. As a coach, I have had the privilege of writing many letters of recommendation for my students in their college application process. Here is a partial list of where some Bayside chess graduates have gone to school:

Rensselaer Polytechnic Institute (RPI)
Harvard University
University of Pennsylvania
Rice
Vanderbilt
Air Force Academy
Merchant Marine Academy
Washington University of St. Louis
Olin College of Engineering

Implementation

Bayside chess works because of a favorable combination of factors that IS repeatable if you are thinking of starting your own chess club. While some might think of Bayside Academy as having certain advantages as a private school, I have seen variations of the model work for inner cities as well as in rural areas. All that is needed is enthusiastic kids, involved parents, supportive administrators, and a passionate leader.

So, you are now convinced of the merits of chess and want to start a program at your school. How do you get started? There are at least three different approaches, all of which can be pursued at the same time, and the right one will depend upon your specific situation.

The first is to organize an after-school club at a school to provide opportunity for those kids who want to play the game. A good first step in approaching the school is identifying a faculty sponsor who is willing to host the activity. A local civic group or other entity can help provide the equipment and even instruction, if there are good chess players in your community. Chess boards and pieces are relatively inexpensive. If several schools in a region start to field teams, arrange competitive matches between the schools as we do in our area. Another way to help schools is to purchase chess software for the school computers so that students can play and learn online.

Another way to start chess interest is by hosting occasional chess tournaments that are open to all. These can be very informal and aimed at the children in a given community. Different sections can be open by age or ability with prizes for each. More equipment, like chess clocks, will be necessary in order for the event to stay on schedule, and this adds to the expense. However, tournaments can also be a great fund raiser for a school or club. At my school we host an annual tournament and the parents chip in to sell food and drinks. Along with the modest entry fees, this allows our club to travel and compete in regional events.

Perhaps the most impactful approach is to talk to your local school board about chess in the curriculum. In my state of Alabama, we are in the second year of a three-year pilot program where the state board of education has selected multiple school systems throughout the state for teaching chess in schools. Teachers were identified and trained over the summer and instruction begins in the fall. You can talk to the chess federation in your state as well as local businesses that rely on math and science majors as a potential funding partners. The advantage of having chess in the curriculum is that all students benefit.

Then, if there is also an extra-curricular program, those who are interested will participate. This is an especially important idea to give chess to all kids because then more girls will play. And, if girls play chess starting at a young age, more are likely to stay with math and science subjects longer in school. If more girls study these subjects longer, more of them are likely to have science, technology, engineering, and math (STEM) majors in college, and the United States will be in position of needing to import fewer engineers from overseas. The potential positive ripple effects of chess in the national education curriculum are enormous.

RESOURCES

These are just some ideas to get started. Here are some resources to help point you in the right direction on your chess journey:

Chess playing web sites
www.chess.com
www.chesskids.com
www.chessclub.com (ICC)

Chess equipment
www.uschess.org
www.cajunchess.com

Chess books to help build a program
Chess for Success by Maurice Ashley

A Beginner's Guide to Coaching Scholastic Chess by Ralph Bowman (e-book)

Checklist for Checkmate: 15 Keys to Building a Successful Team by Eric Nager

Chess Movies

Searching for Bobby Fischer
Knights of the South Bronx
Pawn Sacrifice
The Queen of Katwe
Life of a King
Brooklyn Castle

Curriculum

www.af4c.org American Foundation for Chess

FINAL THOUGHTS

Coaching chess at Bayside Academy has been one of the privileges of my life. The quality of the people there, from the administration to the faculty to the parents, and especially the students, is excellent. Knowing them has enriched me beyond measure.

The quality of excellence at Bayside continuously spurs me to make the chess program excellent, because nothing less will do. If the program stops being excellent, I am no longer interested in being a part of it. By that I do not mean that we have to win all our matches and I do not want to leave the impression that winning is all that matters. An excellent program will win as a byproduct of being excellent. Being excellent means working hard in and outside of practice, committing to your teammates, displaying good sportsmanship, and always learning and growing as a person.

That growth definitely extends to the coach. Coaching chess has helped me in my career by learning to be more patient, seeing the big picture, and devising alternate solutions to problems when the first approach fails. It is also fair to say that different aspects in my career have helped me as a chess coach. For example, my time in the Army taught me leadership and strategic thinking, which comes in pretty handy over the board!

During my time at the school, I believe we have raised the bar on being excellent from competing locally, to statewide, to regionally, to nationally, to internationally. Bayside administrators speak of our program now as a model for other programs, partly because we are co-ed and include all grades from K-12. Part of the fun is finding new ways to raise the bar even higher.

What I am most proud of is the life lessons that have been imparted to the students going through the program. Whether it is lessons on leadership, commitment, punctuality, courtesy, or putting others ahead of self, these lessons will serve the students well in college, in their careers, and beyond. Now here is the funny little secret about imparting these lessons, but you have to promise not to tell anyone else: *they have almost nothing to do with the game of chess. Chess is merely the vehicle for me to be close to these outstanding kids.* Thanks for keeping that between us.

After nineteen years of coaching, the biggest treat is the individual relationships I have developed with the students. It is amazing to me how each respond to different motivators and so I coach every kid in a unique way. My hope is that our relationships turn into friendships when they move on from Bayside and that these friendships will last a lifetime. Then, when I see the student's years from now in different walks of life, we can reminisce about our exploits over the chess board and all the fun we had together.

Epilogue

Where are they now?

Following is a brief summary of where each member of the Bayside National Championship team is today and what they have done since graduation.

Sam Davis graduated from Auburn University in hospitality and now is a general manager for Hilton Hotels.

J.B. Galle graduated from Auburn University and is a film producer, splitting his time between New York City and southern Alabama.

David Gardner graduated from the Olin College of Engineering in Needham, Massachusetts. He then moved to Seattle where he worked for Microsoft and Amazon before becoming a product manager with Luminaire Coffee.

David Mackey graduated from Texas A&M with a degree in computer engineering, and is now a software Engineer for Twitter in the San Francisco Bay area.

Joey Nickerson graduated from Auburn University with a degree in civil engineering and earned a master's in structural engineering. He then moved to Redding, California and graduated from the Bethel School of Supernatural Ministry where he is now an administrator.

Jay Smith was appointed to the Merchant Marine Academy in King's Point, New York. Upon graduation he was commissioned as an ensign in the U.S. Navy Reserve and now works as a ship broker in the Miami, Florida area.

Stephen Smith graduated from the University of South Alabama, majoring in piano performance. He now teaches piano and paints.

APPENDIX

As this book was being written, the first Alabama Chess In School (ACIS) study came out in January of 2019. Authored by professors from Tennessee Tech University and the University of Alabama, it reported on the first three years of the program where chess was in the curriculum in multiple Alabama public schools and, not surprisingly, they show concrete benefits from chess.

Here are some findings from the second section of the report on 21st Century Skills, "The eight skills were academic achievement, affective decision and judgment processes, critical thinking, strategic thinking, problem solving, systems thinking, cross-disciplinary thinking, and overall engagement. Holding other variables constant, students exposed to chess were, on average, consistently rated by their teachers as having made improvements in each of these domains. Chess instruction had the most presumed effect on five constructs: overall engagement, critical thinking, strategic thinking, systems thinking, and problem solving."

"Overall, teachers in the intervention groups (kids taught chess) evaluated their students' 21st Century Skills with higher scores than students in the control groups (kids not taught chess) in the eight skill areas. In Year 3, when compared to the control groups, the intervention students had higher averages in every grade level included in the analysis for the following skills: Affective Decision & Judgment Processes, Systems Thinking, Cross-Disciplinary Thinking, and Overall Engagement."

The full report can be viewed at https://chessinschools.us.

About the Author

Eric M. Nager is an Investment Adviser Representative with Southern Capital Services, Inc. and the first and only Chess Coach (so far) at Bayside Academy, both located in Daphne, Alabama. He has been at both jobs since 2000. At Bayside, his varsity teams have amassed a record of 151-25-29 (.807 winning percentage), to include thirteen local league championships, Seven high school state championships, one junior varsity state championship, two middle school state championships, one elementary state championship, and one national championship in the U1200 rating division. The team has also competed internationally in Russia. Eric graduated from Principia College with a degree in business and history and holds an MBA from the University of South Alabama, where he is an adjunct instructor, as well as a master's in history from Harvard. Eric retired from the U.S. Army Reserve after a thirty-year career, attaining the rank of lieutenant colonel. In his free time, he enjoys spending time with family, reading, traveling, and golf.

He is the married father of two daughters, Nicole and Brooklee, both of whom play chess.

Made in the USA
Columbia, SC
02 January 2020